KEEP ON KNOCKING

DAVID HOPE

All rights reserved. Written permission must be secured from the publisher to use or reproduce any part of this book, except for brief quotations in critical reviews or articles.

Keep On Knocking Copyright 2020 by David Hope

ISBN 978-1-7345273-2-2

Printed in the United States of America.

Rev Media Publishing
PO Box 5172
Kingwood, TX 77325

www.revmediapublishing.com

DEDICATION

I dedicate this book to my wife Sandy. She has continuously demonstrated faithfulness to God and to her family through forty years of marriage. She has taught me the true biblical meaning of continuous knocking for the Lord. Without her love and faithfulness, I could not have written this book.

What Others Are Saying

Keep On Knocking, by David Hope is a concisely written book, addressing all of the spiritual aches and pains of purposeful praying. Hope effectively shows the reader how to treat these chronic pains and frustrations of our prayer life by encouraging an attitude of boldness and perseverance. It is clear that *Keep On Knocking* wastes no time discussing various strategies, biblical and practical, in praying with power, authority, and expectation.

Hope provides us a great service with his compact and literate take on our capacity to be heard by God. One of the most fascinating chapters catalogues the uses of natural and spiritual boldness - underscoring that the power of aggressively directed prayer places heavy emphasis on expecting victorious results in our pursuit of God's ear.

Ultimately, Hope's work emphasizes our attitude and approach to prayer will exact great spiritual success in our dialog with Christ.

—Frank Mazzapica
Pastor, New Covenant Church, Humble TX

Once more David Hope has produced a book of practical "hope" and help for any Christian who has become weak in faith and passive in living. This book, *Keep On Knocking*, will not only strengthen you to rise Up against your spiritual adversity but will also enable you to do so with inner strength and detailed wisdom.

—Bron Barkley, M.A.
D.Min / Director of Alive Ministries / Kingwood, Texas

It is an honor for me to write this recommendation for Pastor David's new book, *Keep On Knocking*. Years ago, I was blessed to be in a small minister's meeting with the late Kenneth Hagin Sr. A pastor asked brother Hagin, " How long do I stand for what I'm believing for"? Without hesitation Papa Hagin answered, "If you are willing to stand forever it won't take very long". Pastor David, with much scripture, shows us that God honors perseverance. If your attitude is – Devil, if you want a fight, then a fight of faith you'll get; then when the dust settles you will still be standing declaring "as for me and my house we will serve the Lord". If you keep on knocking God will answer and you will win. This book shows you how to overcome. It's a must read especially for hungry believers and sincere seekers. Enjoy!

—Dr. Gary Wood,
Evangelist and author of "A Place Called Heaven"

My friend David Hope has once again challenged my thinking with fresh insight into the Living Word. *Keep On Knocking* is a book I highly recommend you read. It speaks clearly and truthfully to every heart that hungers for the fulfillment of God's promises. As he so eloquently states in the book, 'We keep on knocking because we are expecting an answer. We expect an answer because we believe His promise.'

—Winston Hancock
Senior Pastor, Northpark Christian Church, Kingwood, TX

In his introduction of *Keep On Knocking*, David Hope writes, "I am trusting God that as you read this book you will have a greater revelation of kingdom principles. I believe that this book will help you gain the kingdom way of thinking with a godly anticipation of victory as you await answers to prayer and harvests from seeds sown." From the very beginning of his book David reveals his heart-felt desire to share with followers of Christ clear, biblical reasons as to why their prayers sometimes go unanswered. This book will amaze you as he shares with you his thoughts concerning the reasons for our unanswered prayers. His insight may give you a fresh perspective on the subject.

Keep On Knocking is a book concerning prayer but it is much more! David's insights of biblical principles are similar to those of a skillful surgeon. He dissects 'kingdom principles' and gives the reader his spiritual diagnosis and prognosis. His insights cut through the 'sometimes accepted answers' offered as to why believers sometimes don't see results from their prayers. This book offers the reader hope and faith to believe that God not only hears our prayers but also answers them.

You will be carried along from the very beginning through a myriad of scripture; many of which you never thought pertained to the subject of prayer. *Keep On Knocking* is also chock-full of practical experiences of the author and others. Sharing these deeply personal life experiences add to the practical application of the content of this book.

Keep On Knocking will increase the faith of the 'beginner' and the 'mature' saint as well.

I highly recommend that you add this book to your present library. You will treasure it and who knows – you may offer it to a fellow sojourner who is at the same place you once were.

—C. E. Buddy Hicks, D. Min.

INTRODUCTION

The purpose for this book, Keep on Knocking, is to reveal principles of the kingdom of God that relate to receiving answers to prayer. It is not intended to be an all-inclusive teaching on prayer. First of all, I don't even come close to knowing everything there is to know about prayer, but I do know some kingdom principles that relate to prayer and receiving.

I am trusting God that as you read this book you will have a greater revelation of kingdom principles. I believe that this book will help you gain the kingdom way of thinking with a godly anticipation of victory as you await answers to prayer and harvests from seeds sown.

I declare in the name of Jesus that the devil will not steal one seed sown into your hearts from the pages of this book. I decree and establish it by faith that every revelation from the Word of God received from reading this book will produce fruit in your life—fruit that shall remain all the days of your life for the glory of God. I trust that you will enjoy and be blessed!

CHAPTER ONE

PASSIVITY VERSUS BOLDNESS

There is natural boldness and there is a spiritual boldness. Natural boldness is not always good. In fact, it most often manifests as rudeness and selfishness. The type of boldness that we will consider in this chapter is spiritual boldness—contrasting it with spiritual passivity.

Why do we need spiritual boldness? Let's look at Ephesians 6:19-20:

> "And for me, that utterance may be given unto me, that I may open my mouth boldly, to make known the mystery of the gospel, For which I am an ambassador in bonds: that therein I may speak boldly, as I ought to speak." (Ephesians 6:19-20)

We need spiritual boldness to make the mystery of the gospel known as much as we can. The more boldness we have, the more we can spread the gospel. We will learn that passivity in this aspect of our faith brings destruction; boldness brings victory.

> "And it came to pass after these things that Naboth the Jezreelite had a vineyard which was in Jezreel, next to the

palace of Ahab king of Samaria. So Ahab spoke to Naboth, saying, "Give me your vineyard, that I may have it for a vegetable garden, because it is near, next to my house; and for it I will give you a vineyard better than it. Or, if it seems good to you, I will give you its worth in money. "But Naboth said to Ahab, "The LORD forbid that I should give the inheritance of my fathers to you!" So Ahab went into his house sullen and displeased because of the word which Naboth the Jezreelite had spoken to him; for he had said, "I will not give you the inheritance of my fathers." And he lay down on his bed, and turned away his face, and would eat no food. But Jezebel his wife came to him, and said to him, "Why is your spirit so sullen that you eat no food?" He said to her, "Because I spoke to Naboth the Jezreelite, and said to him, 'Give me your vineyard for money; or else, if it pleases you, I will give you another vineyard for it.' And he answered, 'I will not give you my vineyard.'" Then Jezebel his wife said to him, "You now exercise authority over Israel! Arise, eat food, and let your heart be cheerful; I will give you the vineyard of Naboth the Jezreelite." And she wrote letters in Ahab's name, sealed them with his seal, and sent the letters to the elders and the nobles who were dwelling in the city with Naboth. She wrote in the letters, saying, Proclaim a fast, and seat Naboth with high honor among the people; and seat two men, scoundrels, before him to bear witness against him, saying, "You have blasphemed God and the king." Then take him out, and stone him, that he may die. So the men of his city, the elders and nobles who were inhabitants of his city, did as Jezebel had sent to them, as it was written in the letters which she had sent to them. They proclaimed a fast, and seated Naboth with high honor among the people. And two men, scoundrels, came in and sat before him; and the scoundrels witnessed against him, against Naboth, in the presence of the people, saying, "Naboth has blasphemed God and the king!" Then they took him outside the city and stoned him with stones, so that he died. Then they sent to Jezebel, saying, "Naboth has been stoned and is dead." And it came *to pass, when Jezebel heard that Naboth had been stoned and was dead, that Jezebel said to Ahab, "Arise, take possession of the vineyard of Naboth the Jezreelite, which he refused to give you for money; for Naboth is not alive, but dead." So it was, when Ahab heard that Naboth was dead, that Ahab got up and went down to take possession of the vineyard of Naboth the Jezreelite. Then the word of the LORD came to Elijah the Tishbite, saying, "Arise, go down to meet Ahab king of Israel, who lives in Samaria. There he is, in the vineyard of Naboth, where he has gone down to take possession of it. You shall speak to him, saying, 'Thus says the LORD: "Have you murdered and also taken possession?"' And you shall speak to him, saying, 'Thus says the LORD: "In the place where dogs licked the blood of Naboth, dogs shall lick your blood, even yours."' So Ahab said to Elijah, "Have you found me, O my enemy?" And he answered, "I have found you, because you have sold yourself to do evil in the sight of the LORD: 'Behold, I will bring calamity on you. I will take away your posterity, and will cut off from Ahab every male in Israel, both bond and free. I will make your house like the house of Jeroboam the son of Nebat, and like the house of Baasha the son of Ahijah, because of the provocation with which you have provoked Me to anger, and made Israel sin.' And concerning Jezebel the LORD also spoke, saying, 'The dogs shall eat Jezebel by the wall of Jezreel.' The dogs shall eat whoever belongs to Ahab and dies in the city, and the birds of the air shall eat whoever dies in the field." But there was no one like Ahab who sold himself to do wickedness in the sight of the LORD, because Jezebel his wife stirred him up."* (1Kings 21:1-25, NKJV)

Deception works with passivity. They go hand in hand. The deception is that "everything will be alright if you say and do nothing" or "I didn't do anything wrong." Let's continue in the story of Ahab and Jezebel and see how things turn out.

> *"Now when Jehu had come to Jezreel, Jezebel heard of it; and she put paint on her eyes and adorned her head, and looked through a window. Then, as Jehu entered at the gate, she said, "Is it peace, Zimri, murderer of your master?" And he looked up at the window, and said, "Who is on my side? Who?" So two or three eunuchs looked out at him. Then he said, "Throw her down." So they threw her down, and some of her blood spattered on the wall and on the horses; and he trampled her underfoot. And when he had gone in, he ate and drank. Then he said, "Go now, see to this accursed woman, and bury her, for she was a king's daughter." So they went to bury her, but they found no more of her than the skull and the feet and the palms of her hands. Therefore they came back and told him. And he said, "This is the word of the LORD, which He spoke by His servant Elijah the Tishbite, saying, 'On the plot of ground at Jezreel dogs shall eat the flesh of Jezebel; and the corpse of Jezebel shall be as refuse on the surface of the field, in the plot at Jezreel, so that they shall not say, "Here lies Jezebel."'"*
> (2Kings 9:30-37, NKJV)

Things didn't work out too well for Jezebel. Let's see what happened to King Ahab and his seventy sons.

> *"And it came to pass, when the letter came to them, that they took the king's sons, and slew seventy persons, and put their heads in baskets, and sent him them to Jezreel. And there came a messenger, and told him, saying, They have brought the heads of the king's sons. And he said, Lay ye them in two heaps at the entering in of the gate until the morning. And it came to pass in the morning, that he went out, and stood, and said to all the people, Ye be righteous: behold, I conspired against my master, and slew him: but who slew all these? Know now that there shall fall unto the earth nothing of the word of the LORD, which the LORD spake concerning the house of Ahab: for the LORD hath done that which he spake by his servant Elijah. So Jehu slew all that remained*

of the house of Ahab in Jezreel, and all his great men, and his kinsfolks, and his priests, until he left him none remaining." (2 Kings 10:7-11)

King Ahab did not stand up to Jezebel. He was passive. In his mind, he did not do anything wrong. After all, the murder was all Jezebel's idea and he had nothing to do with it. Remember, part of the deception that comes with the sin of passivity is "that everything will work out if I do nothing" and "I haven't done anything wrong." Ahab was king and he had the authority and the responsibility to see that justice was done. He was in a place of spiritual authority, yet he operated in spiritual passivity.

It is true that it was Jezebel's idea, and it was Jezebel who gave the orders, and Ahab's hands did not touch Naboth. Yet in whose face did the prophet of God point his finger, Jezebel's or Ahab's?

"And the word of the LORD came to Elijah the Tishbite, saying, Arise, go down to meet Ahab king of Israel, which is in Samaria: behold, he is in the vineyard of Naboth, whither he is gone down to possess it." (1 Kings 21:17-18)

The deception of passivity is the same deception as in the Garden of Eden. The deception connected to passivity from the enemy triggered man's original sin.

"And God blessed them, and God said unto them, Be fruitful, and multiply, and replenish the earth, and subdue it: and have dominion over the fish of the sea, and over the fowl of the air, and over every living thing that moveth upon the earth. And God said, Behold, I have given you every herb bearing seed, which is upon the face of all the earth, and every tree, in the which is the fruit of a tree yielding seed; to you it shall be for meat. And to every beast of the earth, and to every fowl of the air, and to every thing that creepeth upon the earth,

wherein there is life, I have given every green herb for meat: and it was so." (Genesis 1:28-30)

God gave Adam authority to rule just as Ahab had authority to rule as king. God commanded Adam to rule.

"And the LORD God commanded the man, saying, Of every tree of the garden thou mayest freely eat: But of the tree of the knowledge of good and evil, thou shalt not eat of it: for in the day that thou eatest thereof thou shalt surely die." (Genesis 2:16-17)

God commanded the man Adam. It does not say that God commanded the woman or Eve or the man and the woman. At this point, the woman was not yet manifested. God gave the man Adam spiritual authority. Adam had the spiritual responsibility to make sure that God's instructions were followed. Because of the passivity of Adam, the first sin appeared on the earth. God's kingdom was no longer on earth as it was in heaven.

"And when the woman saw that the tree was good for food, and that it was pleasant to the eyes, and a tree to be desired to make one wise, she took of the fruit thereof, and did eat, and gave also unto her husband with her; and he did eat." (Genesis 3:6)

The basis of passivity is fear. Adam was afraid that Eve wouldn't love him if he operated in his spiritual authority to lovingly stop her from eating of the forbidden fruit. He could have told her that because of his great love for her he must protect her by keeping her in obedience to God. Instead, he desired to please Eve more than he desired to please God.

After all, Eve was so beautiful. She was even more beautiful than Jezebel. Can you imagine how overwhelmed with love and delight Adam must have been when he first laid his eyes on Eve?

> "And the LORD God caused a deep sleep to fall upon Adam and he slept: and he took one of his ribs, and closed up the flesh instead thereof; And the rib, which the LORD God had taken from man, made he a woman, and brought her unto the man. And Adam said, This is now bone of my bones, and flesh of my flesh: she shall be called Woman, because she was taken out of Man." (Genesis 2:21-23)

Adam was formed but Eve was built. The fear of losing Eve's love caused Adam to be passive and fail to exercise spiritual boldness. Fear produces passivity. Adam was afraid that Eve wouldn't love him. Ahab was afraid that Jezebel wouldn't love him, so he was passive and failed to exercise his God-given authority.

Parents often are afraid to train and discipline their children for fear of losing their love, even though God requires them to do so. Parents have God-given spiritual authority and responsibility to discipline their children, yet fear often stops them. They are afraid of losing their children's love.

If parents will train and discipline their children according to God's instructions, their children will love them more. If Adam had spoken the truth in love to Eve, she would have loved him all the more. If Ahab had stood up to Jezebel, he would have avoided the loss of his posterity and the tragic, untimely death of Jezebel. We must love God enough to overcome our fears. Such love produces trust and faith, which brings obedience. Loving God more, we will love our spouse and children more. The more we are faithful to God, the more we will be faithful to each other.

Why are we reviewing what happened to Adam and Eve and Ahab and Jezebel? After all, those things happened so long ago. The reality is, these principles hold true today because Jesus, the Truth, never changes. What was true then is true now.

"Jesus Christ the same yesterday, and today, and forever." (Hebrews 13:8)

"For I am the LORD, I change not." (Malachi 3:6)

To illustrate the principle that what is true in one time holds true in another time, let's look at a modern-day Jezebel. Let's see how it ended for an evil, "Jezebel type" woman today. The following contains excerpts from an Associated Press article by Jim Vertuno that appeared in the January 29, 2001 Houston Chronicle. According to his report, all that was left of Madalyn Murray O'Hair was her skull, an artificial hip, and the palms of her hands.

Investigators pulled more human remains, including a metal artificial hip bone and three skulls, from the ground Sunday at a South Texas ranch, bolstering their belief that they have finally solved the mystery of what happened to Madalyn Murray O'Hair and her two children, missing since 1995…

"The bones indicate three sets of human remains," [FBI special agent Roderick] Beverly said. *"All appeared to have their legs cut off. The remains and the ground around the bones were charred, indicating a fire at the scene."*

Prosecutors contend the victims were dismembered at a public storage shed in Austin, placed in 55-gallon drums and dumped on the ranch…David Glassman, chairman of the anthropology department at Southwest Texas State University, said a skull and a pair of hands were found buried away from the other bodies in the pit. The skull and hands were in a plastic bag with some clothing…O'Hair enjoyed calling herself the most hated woman in America. She was involved in successful court battles in the 1960's to ban prayer and Bible reading in the nation's public schools.

Spiritual passivity driven by fear is still operating in the body of Christ today. If this deception is not resisted, passivity will cause us to quit striving toward our spiritual destiny and produce all kinds of havoc in our lives and in the lives of those we love.

Let's look at areas of our lives that need to be inspected for the deception of passivity. For example, let's examine the relationship between husbands and wives. Husbands should be the spiritual leader of the home. If the husband is passive in this role, it can cause problems. Wives should always encourage their husbands to take this role, even if the husband is not strong spiritually. Wives should make their husbands feel like they are spiritual giants and then watch them grow into just that. If a man is passive in that role, it can lead to an unhappy marriage and even divorce. Then each spouse will not only lose each other but both will also suffer a great financial loss. In addition, the greatest loss of all occurs in the life of any children involved.

When parents, especially fathers, are passive in the responsibility of disciplining and training up of a child, problems ensue. Remember, the deception that goes hand-in-hand with passivity is that if you do nothing, everything will work out fine. This notion is contrary to God's Word.

"The rod and reproof give wisdom: but a child left to himself bringeth his mother to shame." (Proverbs. 29:15)

The result of passive parenting is rebellion of the child toward parents and toward God. How can children submit to God who they can't see if they can't submit to parents they can see? Parents are to take bold steps to train their children to honor the word and the voice of their parents. Then when they grow up, they will honor the Word and the voice of God.

Many times, business owners or managers and heads of ministries won't address problems they see because they hope that things will just work out on their own. I can tell you from experience that rarely happens. When you ignore things, they don't go away. The only things that go away if you ignore them are your teeth! The earlier that you deal with a problem, the easier it is to solve. If you have been given the authority and the responsibility to oversee an operation, then passivity won't work. You don't have to be abrasive in dealing with people who need help or direction. In a spirit of meekness, you can speak the truth in love.

If problems are not addressed due to passivity, a business can go under, and a ministry can also go under, due to a breach in integrity or financial oversights. When bosses are more afraid of not being liked than they are of poor performance, passivity will set in. The truth is that you are actually serving your employees when you help them perform at a higher level. You must be a true servant so that your boldness to instruct is seen as an act of love and service. Employees must know that you care for them. This will produce higher productivity.

> *"Servants, be obedient to them that are your masters according to the flesh, with fear and trembling, in singleness of your heart, as unto Christ; And, ye masters, do the same things unto them, forbearing threatening: knowing that your Master also is in heaven; neither is there respect of persons with him. Finally, my brethren, be strong in the Lord, and in the power of his might."* (Ephesians 6:5, 9-10)

Passivity is also a big problem in government, especially in the United States. People who have been given authority and responsibility by the voters stand idly by and watch our beloved country's founding principles and liberties diminish. Oh, there might be some saber rattling, but very few have the courage to speak the truth.

Why are they so passive? They are more afraid of losing an election than doing their constitutional duty. Passivity is always linked to fear and deception. They do nothing, thinking it won't end up so badly and they can still get elected. That's not serving the people!

We need someone who serves God and can discern the truth by the Spirit of God and stand up to Muslim extremists, union thugs, communists, Fabian socialists, Marxists, the new Black Panthers, and people like George Soros. Many of those trying to destroy our nation by stripping away our liberties already hold high positions in our federal government. There is no time left for passivity! Passivity is not of God and it brings destruction. The result of passivity in government is loss of liberties.

Spiritual passivity can also make us afraid to share the gospel. The fear of rejection causes us to do nothing, hoping that everything will somehow work out. Perhaps someone else will share the gospel with them. Passivity toward obeying God may also manifest in the holding back of a word of wisdom, a word of knowledge, or cause someone not to release a prophecy from the Lord.

Passivity occurs because of the fear of rejection. The result of such passivity is to give the devil a foothold in a household or a community. The result of the boldness to speak what the Spirit of the Lord is saying is to set free a household or a community.

Jesus was not passive. He always chose the path of boldness.

> *"And Jesus went into the temple of God, and cast out all them that sold and bought in the temple, and overthrew the tables of the moneychangers, and the seats of them that sold doves, And said unto them, It is written, My house shall be called the house of prayer; but ye have made it a den of thieves."* (Matthew 21:12-13)

> *"But when he saw many of the Pharisees and Sadducees*

come to his baptism, he said unto them, O generation of vipers, who hath warned you to flee from the wrath to come? Bring forth therefore fruits meet for repentance." (Matthew 3:7-8)

Jesus told the people that hell was real. He didn't let passivity hold him back. He spoke the truth in love.

"And fear not them which kill the body, but are not able to kill the soul: but rather fear him which is able to destroy both soul and body in hell. Are not two sparrows sold for a farthing? and one of them shall not fall on the ground without your Father. But the very hairs of your head are all numbered. Fear ye not therefore, ye are of more value than many sparrows. Whosoever therefore shall confess me before men, him will I confess also before my Father which is in heaven. But whosoever shall deny me before men, him will I also deny before my Father which is in heaven. Think not that I am come to send peace on earth: I came not to send peace, but a sword. For I am come to set a man at variance against his father, and the daughter against her mother, and the daughter in law against her mother in law. And a man's foes shall be they of his own household. He that loveth father or mother more than me is not worthy of me: and he that loveth son or daughter more than me is not worthy of me And he that taketh not his cross, and followeth after me, is not worthy of me. He that findeth his life shall lose it: and he that loseth his life for my sake shall find it." (Matthew 10:28-39)

God wants us to be bold for the cause of Christ. As we operate in love, the more boldness is released and more good fruit is produced. After Peter told the Jews that they hung the Messiah on a tree, 3,000 people were saved. The spirit of fear (timidity or passivity) is not from God.

"For God hath not given us the spirit of fear; but of power, and of love, and of a sound mind." (2 Timothy 1:7)

Let's see how Peter operated when preaching to the Jews.

> "Therefore let all the house of Israel know assuredly, that God hath made that same Jesus, whom ye have crucified, both Lord and Christ. Now when they heard this, they were pricked in their heart, and said unto Peter and to the rest of the apostles, Men and brethren, what shall we do? Then Peter said unto them, Repent, and be baptized every one of you in the name of Jesus Christ for the remission of sins, and ye shall receive the gift of the Holy Ghost. For the promise is unto you, and to your children, and to all that are afar off, even as many as the Lord our God shall call. And with many other words did he testify and exhort, saying, Save yourselves from this untoward generation. Then they that gladly received his word were baptized: and the same day there were added unto them about three thousand souls." (Acts 2:36-41)

Imagine what would have happened to those 3,000 souls if Peter would have said "Why rock the boat, everything will work out fine if we do nothing. We don't have to tell them what they've done."

Instead of backing off, Peter got even bolder in the Holy Ghost.

> "And as the lame man which was healed held Peter and John, all the people ran together unto them in the porch that is called Solomon's, greatly wondering. And when Peter saw it, he answered unto the people, Ye men of Israel, why marvel ye at this? or why look ye so earnestly on us, as though by our own power or holiness we had made this man to walk? The God of Abraham, and of Isaac, and of Jacob, the God of our fathers, hath glorified his Son Jesus; whom ye delivered up, and denied him in the presence of Pilate, when he was determined to let him go. But ye denied the Holy One and the Just, and desired a murderer to be granted unto you; And killed the Prince of life, whom God hath raised from the dead; whereof

we are witnesses. And his name through faith in his name hath made this man strong, whom ye see and know: yea, the faith which is by him hath given him this perfect soundness in the presence of you all. And now, brethren, I wot that through ignorance ye did it, as did also your rulers. But those things, which God before had shewed by the mouth of all his prophets, that Christ should suffer, he hath so fulfilled. Repent ye therefore, and be converted, that your sins may be blotted out, when the times of refreshing shall come from the presence of the Lord." (Acts 3:11-19)

The result of that act of boldness brought 5,000 souls into the kingdom of God.

"Howbeit many of them which heard the word believed; and the number of the men was about five thousand." (Acts 4:4)

The boldness of the Holy Ghost is stronger than the deception of passivity from the devil. Peter and John kept declaring the mystery of the gospel with boldness.

"And Annas the high priest, and Caiaphas, and John, and Alexander, and as many as were of the kindred of the high priest, were gathered together at Jerusalem. And when they had set them in the midst, they asked, By what power, or by what name, have ye done this? Then Peter, filled with the Holy Ghost, said unto them, Ye rulers of the people, and elders of Israel, If we this day be examined of the good deed done to the impotent man, by what means he is made whole; Be it known unto you all, and to all the people of Israel, that by the name of Jesus Christ of Nazareth, whom ye crucified, whom God raised from the dead, even by him doth this man stand here before you whole. This is the stone which was set at nought of you builders, which is become the head of the corner. Neither is there salvation in any other: for there is none other name under heaven given among men, whereby we

must be saved. Now when they saw the boldness of Peter and John, and perceived that they were unlearned and ignorant men, they marvelled; and they took knowledge of them, that they had been with Jesus. And beholding the man which was healed standing with them, they could say nothing against it. So when they had further threatened them, they let them go, finding nothing how they might punish them, because of the people: for all men glorified God for that which was done." (Acts 4:6-14, 21)

How did Peter and John get this boldness? Let's see what the Scriptures reveal.

"And now, Lord, behold their threatenings: and grant unto thy servants, that with all boldness they may speak thy word, By stretching forth thine hand to heal; and that signs and wonders may be done by the name of thy holy child Jesus. And when they had prayed, the place was shaken where they were assembled together; and they were all filled with the Holy Ghost, and they spake the word of God with boldness." (Acts 4:29-31)

Passivity lets the devil have dominion. Boldness in the Holy Ghost makes the devil do nothing. Boldness scares the devil.

"Now when they saw the boldness of Peter and John, and perceived that they were unlearned and ignorant men, they marvelled; and they took knowledge of them, that they had been with Jesus. And beholding the man which was healed standing with them, they could say nothing against it." (Acts 4:13-14)

The devil can say nothing against boldness. In fact, persecution just brought an opportunity for more demonstration of power and release of the gospel. Boldness brings the power of God. God has boldness with power. The devil brings passivity with deception. Let's see how power was manifested as a result of the boldness of Peter and John.

> *"And believers were the more added to the Lord, multitudes both of men and women.) Insomuch that they brought forth the sick into the streets, and laid them on beds and couches, that at the least the shadow of Peter passing by might overshadow some of them. There came also a multitude out of the cities round about unto Jerusalem, bringing sick folks, and them which were vexed with unclean spirits: and they were healed every one."* (Acts 5:14-16)

Such amazing power comes from unconditionally believing what God has said. We will not fear man because we are convinced that God is always for us and not against us. We can concentrate on obeying God without fear of what man will do. That is the key to godly boldness. This can only come from an intimate encounter with a holy God. We don't fret over our mistakes. We boldly approach God because we are not afraid of him.

We should always run to God, especially when we have messed up. It's then more than ever that we need mercy. Where else can we go to find more mercy than from God whose mercies are new every morning? We trust God because we believe he is not a liar.

"Let your conversation be without covetousness; and be content with such things as ye have: for he hath said, I will never leave thee, nor forsake thee. So that we may boldly say, The Lord is my helper, and I will not fear what man shall do unto me." (Hebrews 13:5-6)

> *"Seeing then that we have a great high priest, that is passed into the heavens, Jesus the Son of God, let us hold fast our profession. For we have not an high priest which cannot be touched with the feeling of our infirmities; but was in all points*

> *tempted like as we are, yet without sin. Let us therefore come boldly unto the throne of grace, that we may obtain mercy, and find grace to help in time of need."* (Hebrews 4:14-16)

If we want to go into the world to proclaim Jesus with boldness, we must go to his throne room with boldness. The more boldness we have to approach God's throne the more boldness we will manifest in demonstrating God to this world. We cannot approach God if we are afraid of him. I'm not talking about the fear of God as in a reverential awe and respect. I'm talking about fear as in a phobia, the kind we receive from the enemy.

God wants us to approach him boldly as if we believe that we are his children and joint heirs with Jesus. In other words, we believe what he has said. The more boldly we approach God in secret, the more open our boldness will be before men.

How do we receive boldness? First, we ask for it. Peter and John asked God to grant them more godly boldness. Then, go to God in secret with boldness and you will have boldness openly in the world. Then use the boldness God gives you because everything you use for God comes back with increase.

Finally, understand that you receive it by faith. Everything you receive from God comes by grace through faith. We don't have to earn it. We are then free to love others because we are not afraid. We receive God's love and boldness to proclaim the gospel. We are not afraid because the punishment we deserve was given to Jesus, the Lamb of God. Don't be afraid and think that you must "get cleaned up" before you go to God. Seek God and then he will clean you up. Only he can do that.

> *"Herein is our love made perfect, that we may have boldness in the day of judgment: because as he is, so are we in this world. There is no fear in love; but perfect love casteth out*

fear: because fear hath torment. He that feareth is not made perfect in love. We love him, because he first loved us. And this commandment have we from him, That he who loveth God love his brother also." (1 John 4:17-19, 21)

. *"All we like sheep have gone astray; we have turned every one to his own way; and the LORD hath laid on him the iniquity of us all."* (Isaiah 53:6)

"For God hath not appointed us to wrath, but to obtain salvation by our Lord Jesus Christ." (1 Thessalonians 5:9)

CHAPTER TWO

KEEP ON KNOCKING

If we keep on knocking on God's door, is that natural boldness or is that spiritual boldness? Is it a lack of faith to keep on praying when we don't see an answer? Jesus says no. In fact, Jesus equates persistence with faith. Continued knocking is spiritual boldness.

> "Ask, and it shall be given you; seek, and ye shall find; knock, and it shall be opened unto you: For every one that asketh receiveth; and he that seeketh findeth; and to him that knocketh it shall be opened. Or what man is there of you, whom if his son ask bread, will he give him a stone? Or if he ask a fish, will he give him a serpent? If ye then, being evil, know how to give good gifts unto your children, how much more shall your Father which is in heaven give good things to them that ask him?" (Matthew 7:7-11)

The three verbs used by Jesus (ask, seek and knock) are used in the Greek present imperative tense. This implies a continuous action. These verbs, if properly translated, should say continue asking, continue seeking, and continue knocking. In other words, keep on asking, keep on seeking, and keep on knocking, because everyone who keeps asking receives, everyone who keeps seeking finds, and to everyone who keeps on knocking it will be opened.

You have to be more determined to receive from God than the devil is determined to stop the blessing. If you don't quit, you will win. Patience or perseverance is one of the fruits of the spirit listed in book of Galatians chapter five. These fruits can only be manifested through the Spirit of God. Since the devil has no Spirit of God in him, he cannot manifest patience. If you keep persevering, the devil will give up and move on.

When you feel like quitting, hold on because Satan wants to quit more than you do. That's why when you get close to the victory, he always make one last big push to make you quit because he can't hang on much longer. Keep knocking and the victory is yours.

Remember, all you need to win a spiritual battle is persistence. Just don't quit. Do you know how much talent, spiritual gifts, and abilities it takes to win a spiritual battle? Let me answer that with more questions. How much ability does it take to not quit? How much gifting does it take to not quit? How much talent does it take to not quit? The answer to all those questions is the same—none!

Anyone can win because anyone can decide that he won't quit. Don't quit and you will win. When you are tempted to give up, keep holding on. Keep on asking, keep on seeking, and keep on knocking.

> "There hath no temptation taken you but such as is common to man: but God is faithful, who will not suffer you to be tempted above that ye are able; but will with the temptation also make a way to escape, that ye may be able to bear it."
> (1 Corinthians 10:13)

The race is not won by the swiftest or the strongest, but the race is won by those who won't quit.

> *"I returned, and saw under the sun, that the race is not to the swift, nor the battle to the strong, neither yet bread to the wise, nor yet riches to men of understanding, nor yet favour to men of skill; but time and chance happeneth to them all."* (Ecclesiastes 9:11)

> *"For ye have need of patience, that, after ye have done the will of God, ye might receive the promise."* (Hebrews 10:36)

A good example of persistence or patience can be seen in the life of Abraham Lincoln. Lincoln lost eight elections. He only won three, including the presidency. He started two businesses and both of them failed. He suffered a nervous breakdown and was in bed for six months. He applied for law school and was rejected. Lincoln never quit and became, in the view of many, the greatest president in the history of the United States of America.

Another good example of perseverance can be seen in the life of Walt Disney. As a young man, Disney was fired from the Kansas City Star newspaper. He was fired because his boss thought he lacked creativity. Disney was forced to shut down his first film company due to financial difficulties, but Walt Disney never quit. Disney's greatest example of perseverance came in the making of the film Mary Poppins. In 1944, Disney asked the author, Pamela Travers, to sell him the rights to make a screen play of the book. Travers had no interest in such a venture. In an attempt to win her over, Disney took trips to Travers' home in England repeatedly for the next 16 years. Disney kept knocking and the film Mary Poppins became a timeless classic for many generations to enjoy. The Disney Company purchased ABC in 1996. At the time, ABC owned the Kansas City Star newspaper. The newspaper that fired Disney had become part of the empire that he created.

Let's look at some biblical examples of persistence or examples of those who kept on knocking.

> *"And he said unto them, Which of you shall have a friend, and shall go unto him at midnight, and say unto him, Friend, lend me three loaves; For a friend of mine in his journey is come to me, and I have nothing to set before him? And he from within shall answer and say, Trouble me not: the door is now shut, and my children are with me in bed; I cannot rise and give thee. I say unto you, though he will not rise and give him, because he is his friend, yet because of his importunity he will rise and give him as many as he needeth. And I say unto you, Ask, and it shall be given you; seek, and ye shall find; knock, and it shall be opened unto you. For every one that asketh receiveth; and he that seeketh findeth; and to him that knocketh it shall be opened. If a son shall ask bread of any of you that is a father, will he give him a stone? or if he ask a fish, will he for a fish give him a serpent? Or if he shall ask an egg, will he offer him a scorpion? If ye then, being evil, know how to give good gifts unto your children: how much more shall your heavenly Father give the Holy Spirit to them that ask him?"* (Luke 11:5-13)

The man would not rise even though his neighbor was his friend. He arose and gave his neighbor as many loaves as he needed because of his neighbor's persistence. In other words, his neighbor kept on knocking, the door was opened, and his need was met.

Likewise, our heavenly Father is never tired and always wants to give to us.

> *"Fear not, little flock; for it is your Father's good pleasure to give you the kingdom."* (Luke 12:32)

Let's look at another powerful example from Jesus that demonstrates to us how important it is to not quit and keep on knocking.

> *"And he spake a parable unto them to this end, that men*

ought always to pray, and not to faint; Saying, There was in a city a judge, which feared not God, neither regarded man: And there was a widow in that city; and she came unto him, saying, Avenge me of mine adversary. And he would not for a while: but afterward he said within himself, Though I fear not God, nor regard man; Yet because this widow troubleth me, I will avenge her, lest by her continual coming she weary me. And the Lord said, Hear what the unjust judge saith. And shall not God avenge his own elect, which cry day and night unto him, though he bear long with them? I tell you that he will avenge them speedily. Nevertheless when the Son of man cometh, shall he find faith on the earth?" (Luke 18:1-8)

The unjust judge had no desire to please God and did not care what men thought about him. He had no desire to act justly or do what was right. The only reason he ruled for justice for the widow was that he knew that she would just keep coming and wear him out unless he gave her justice against her adversary. Continually knocking causes even unjust men to do right. Can you imagine what it will do to a just God who already desires to give you more than you deserve?

God greatly desires to give you more than you deserve. I don't want what I deserve; I'd rather have the grace (unmerited favor) of God.

"Now unto him that is able to do exceeding abundantly above all that we ask or think, according to the power that worketh in us." (Ephesians 3:20)

Jesus has instructed us through the parable of the unjust judge to continue knocking because he considers that as faith and faith is what pleases God. In other words, God is pleased when we continue asking, continue seeking, and continue knocking. Our persistence doesn't just work on our sleepy neighbor or an unjust judge but also on God

Almighty! Persistent knocking works on everyone.

I'll never forget when my wife, Sandy, wanted to have some remodeling done and build an addition to our home. I told her, in no uncertain terms, to forget about it, for there was no way that was going to happen. I played every card in the deck to make sure that it would never happen. I played the "spiritual head of the home" card. I played the "I am an MBA and have done a financial analysis" card. I played the "bunch of dust and what a mess" card. I put forth every possible argument against the idea and declared them with such a ring of authority and finality that no one could possibly think I could ever change my mind and give in. No one could have believed I would consent, except for my wife.

She believed and she never quit. She kept on knocking and knocking and knocking. She got her addition. In fact, she got three more remodels as of this writing. I agreed to the last one joyfully without any resistance. God used my wife, Sandy, to teach me the principle of continuous knocking.

If God says you can have something, don't let anyone else (even loved ones and those in authority) talk you out of it. The only real authority on any subject is the Word of God. The authority of the Word trumps every other authority.

Milwaukee Braves minor league manager Tommy Holmes said the following about Hank Aaron in 1952: "That kid can't play baseball."

Grand Ole Opry manager Jim Denny said the following about Elvis Presley in 1954 after Presley's first performance: "You ain't going nowhere, son. You ought to go back driving a truck."

A Munich teacher said the following to ten-year-old Albert Einstein in 1889: "You will never amount to very much."

Others may tell you to stop believing or stop talking about your dreams. They may want you to quit knocking. Most of the time, they just want to "help" you and keep you from getting hurt. Even though they may be well meaning, and even though they may be an authority, remember that Jesus, the Word of God, has all authority.

> "And Jesus came and spake unto them, saying, All power is given unto me in heaven and in earth." (Matthew 28:18)

> "And it came to pass, when Jesus had ended these sayings, the people were astonished at his doctrine: For he taught them as one having authority, and not as the scribes." (Matthew 7:28-29)

Faith always pleases God. God is pleased when you press in to receive his promise despite opposition. Quitting doesn't please God, for without faith it is impossible to please him.

> "And a woman having an issue of blood twelve years, which had spent all her living upon physicians, neither could be healed of any, Came behind him, and touched the border of his garment: and immediately her issue of blood stanched. And Jesus said, Who touched me? When all denied, Peter and they that were with him said, Master, the multitude throng thee and press thee, and sayest thou, Who touched me? And Jesus said, Somebody hath touched me: for I perceive that virtue is gone out of me. And when the woman saw that she was not hid, she came trembling, and falling down before him, she declared unto him before all the people for what cause she had touched him and how she was healed immediately. And he said unto her, Daughter, be of good comfort: thy faith hath made thee whole; go in peace." (Luke 8:43-48)

Continuous knocking, or pressing in against opposition, brings the answer from God. Your mind may say it's too late; others may say it's impossible. But if you keep on knocking, the door will be open. This woman with the issue of blood pressed in despite the fact that the multitude thronged him and pressed him. Jesus called that faith, and said that her faith had made her whole. In other words, she was made whole because she pressed in to touch him despite opposition.

> *"And they came to Jericho: and as he went out of Jericho with his disciples and a great number of people, blind Bartimaeus, the son of Timaeus, sat by the highway side begging. And when he heard that it was Jesus of Nazareth, he began to cry out, and say, Jesus, thou Son of David, have mercy on me. And many charged him that he should hold his peace: but he cried the more a great deal, Thou Son of David, have mercy on me. And Jesus stood still, and commanded him to be called. And they call the blind man, saying unto him, Be of good comfort, rise; he calleth thee. And he, casting away his garment, rose, and came to Jesus. And Jesus answered and said unto him, What wilt thou that I should do unto thee? The blind man said unto him, Lord, that I might receive my sight. And Jesus said unto him, Go thy way; thy faith hath made thee whole. And immediately he received his sight, and followed Jesus in the way."* (Mark 10:46-52)

Bartimaeus kept knocking when people said give up, be quiet. In fact, when he was told to shut up he cried out a great deal more. When he pressed in even more when opposition came, he got the attention of Jesus. The Bible says, "Jesus stood still, and commanded him to be called." Jesus was so pleased by his continuous knocking that he asked Bartimaeus what is was that he could do for him. Jesus judged his persistence as faith and said that this persistence called faith made him whole.

One of the greatest biblical examples of the miracle workings of continuous prayer was when an angel broke Peter out of prison. Peter's release, prompted by continuous knocking, also demonstrated additional benefits from this godly kingdom principle. Let's see what happened.

> *"Peter therefore was kept in prison: but prayer was made*

without ceasing of the church unto God for him. And when Herod would have brought him forth, the same night Peter was sleeping between two soldiers, bound with two chains: and the keepers before the door kept the prison. And, behold, the angel of the Lord came upon him, and a light shined in the prison: and he smote Peter on the side, and raised him up, saying, Arise up quickly. And his chains fell off from his hands. And the angel said unto him, Gird thyself, and bind on thy sandals. And so he did. And he saith unto him, Cast thy garment about thee, and follow me. And he went out, and followed him; and wist not that it was true which was done by the angel; but thought he saw a vision. When they were past the first and the second ward, they came unto the iron gate that leadeth unto the city; which opened to them of his own accord: and they went out, and passed on through one street; and forthwith the angel departed from him. And when Peter was come to himself, he said, Now I know of a surety, that the Lord hath sent his angel, and hath delivered me out of the hand of Herod, and from all the expectation of the people of the Jews. And when he had considered the thing, he came to the house of Mary the mother of John, whose surname was Mark; where many were gathered together praying. And as Peter knocked at the door of the gate, a damsel came to hearken, named Rhoda. And when she knew Peter's voice, she opened not the gate for gladness, but ran in, and told how Peter stood before the gate. And they said unto her, Thou art mad. But she constantly affirmed that it was even so. Then said they, It is his angel. But Peter continued knocking: and when they had opened the door, and saw him, they were astonished." (Acts 12: 5-16)

They prayed without ceasing. They kept on knocking. This kingdom principle of persistence always generates results. The angel of the Lord was sent and set Peter free. When Peter reached Mary's house, many were there praying that Peter be released from prison. When Peter showed up, they couldn't receive the miracle. In fact, when Rhoda told them that Peter was there, they replied that Rhoda must be crazy. They didn't recognize and receive the miracle because they had expected something else. They thought that the manifestation of the answer to their prayer would come a different way.

How many miracles have passed us by because we expected them to manifest in a way that made sense to our natural mind? God usually answers our requests in a different but much better way than what we anticipate. We should believe God for the miracle but allow God to do it his way. His ways are not our ways. If we are focused on a specific way, then we are in great jeopardy of not recognizing the miracle and letting it pass us by.

I have good news for you. Even if we mess up and don't recognize our miracle, we don't have to lose it. You won't lose it if you keep on knocking! Isn't that what happened to the praying church knocking for Peter's safe return?

If we don't quit, we not only have the principle of persistence working for us, we also have the principle of sowing and reaping working for us as well. If the seed (prayer request) keeps knocking then the harvest (answer) keeps knocking. The answer passed them by. What did they do? They continued praying, they continued knocking. So if the prayer keeps knocking, therefore the answer keeps knocking.

Peter was the answer. When Rhoda told them about Peter and they still didn't believe, what happened? The answer, Peter standing free, continued knocking.

> "But Peter continued knocking." (Acts 12:16)

This incident demonstrates the power God has made available to us if we keep on seeking, keep on asking, and keep on knocking. Why does God classify perseverance as faith? Why is he pleased with us when we keep on knocking? We keep on knocking because we are expecting an answer. We are expecting an answer because we believe his promise, and that's what pleases God. When I believe a promise from God, I expect to receive an answer. When I don't see an answer today, then all the more I am expecting it the next day. With each day that passes, I am closer to the answer and my expectation level rises. I keep speaking that which I want to manifest until I see it in the natural. Then I stop speaking it, because the answer is manifest, the door was opened. When I first spoke, the promise was done, but I keep speaking, keep knocking until the door is opened.

Suppose someone who loves you invites you to his home. He loves you and will be glad to see you when you arrive. He promised you that if you come at a certain time, he would be home. Also imagine that he always keeps his promises. When you arrive at his home, you knock on the door. What do you do if he doesn't answer right away? Do you get in the car and drive away or do you keep on knocking? Of course, you keep on knocking, because you know that he wants to open the door and will be glad to see you.

You keep on knocking because you expect his promise to be good. If he doesn't open the door right away, you don't stop, you knock even louder. Isn't that what blind Bartimaeus did? They told him to be quiet, but he cried out even louder and Jesus said that his faith had made him whole.

You can't lose if you don't quit. The only way to lose is quit. You may be thinking that it's too late because you have already quit. Get back up and starting knocking and keep on knocking until you have the victory. If you are still breathing, it's not too late with God.

> "For a just man falleth seven times, and riseth up again." (Proverbs 24:16)

> "And let us not be weary in well doing: for in due season we shall reap, if we faint not." (Galatians 6:9)

CHAPTER THREE

EXPECT FAST RESULTS

The story of the unjust judge showed us why we can expect fast results from God. In the parable of the unjust judge, Jesus said that God will avenge his elect speedily. This is the normal way God operates. The words most often used to explain the timing of miracles in Jesus' ministry are immediately, straightway, and from that very hour.

How does such a notion connect with faith and patience? To be sure, a battle is necessary for us to possess the promises of God. There are still giants in the land mightier than we are, but the good news is that God has already given us the land. All we have to do is walk in the promises. For the promises of God are more real than the natural land of promise.

> *"Hear, O Israel: Thou art to pass over Jordan this day, to go in to possess nations greater and mightier than thyself, cities great and fenced up to heaven, A people great and tall, the children of the Anakims, whom thou knowest, and of whom thou hast heard say, Who can stand before the children of Anak! Understand therefore this day, that the LORD thy God is he which goeth over before thee; as a consuming fire he shall*

> *destroy them, and he shall bring them down before thy face: so shalt thou drive them out, and destroy them quickly, as the LORD hath said unto thee."* (Deuteronomy 9:1-3)

We shall win the battle quickly. We expect fast results. We have to fight the battle, but we fight the fight of faith. Our part is to believe the promise and speak it, and God does all the work. We do the speaking and God always makes our triumph manifest.

> *"Believest thou not that I am in the Father, and the Father in me? the words that I speak unto you I speak not of myself: but the Father that dwelleth in me, he doeth the works."* (John 14:10)

> *"Now thanks be unto God, which always causeth us to triumph in Christ, and maketh manifest the savour of his knowledge by us in every place."* (2 Corinthians 2:14)

We should always be looking for our answer right away so that it won't pass us by. If we don't see it, we keep on knocking and keep on expecting it to manifest. If we keep knocking, our faith and expectations grow, instead of diminishing, as we wait. The longer we wait, the closer we are to the answer. This is real biblical patience.

As we wait with a spirit of expectation, we still rejoice if the answer tarries. If we are truly expecting fast results in faith, then we know the delay means even a greater victory. If you make a bank deposit, isn't the amount greater the longer you wait before withdrawal? The longer you wait, the more interest, or increase, is added. Abraham waited a long time and look how great the manifestation of his promise turned out. Meditate on how long God the Father had to wait for the physical, natural birth of God the Son and the far-reaching, wonderful blessings that resulted.

"But when the fulness of the time was come, God sent forth his Son, made of a woman, made under the law, To redeem them that were under the law, that we might receive the adoption of sons. And because ye are sons, God hath sent forth the Spirit of his Son into your hearts, crying, Abba, Father. Wherefore thou art no more a servant, but a son; and if a son, then an heir of God through Christ." (Galatians 4:4-7)

Consider the following verse:

"And it shall be, when the LORD thy God shall have brought thee into the land which he sware unto thy fathers, to Abraham, to Isaac, and to Jacob, to give thee great and goodly cities, which thou buildedst not, And houses full of all good things, which thou filledst not, and wells digged, which thou diggedst not, vineyards and olive trees, which thou plantedst not; when thou shalt have eaten and be full." (Deuteronomy 6:10-11)

If the children of Israel had not listened to the evil reports, but instead listened to Joshua and Caleb, they could have entered the Promised Land after approximately thirteen months in the wilderness. The adults (besides Joshua and Caleb) could not enter because of their unbelief.

"But with whom was he grieved forty years? was it not with them that had sinned, whose carcases fell in the wilderness? And to whom sware he that they should not enter into his rest, but to them that believed not? So we see that they could not enter in because of unbelief," (Hebrews 3:17-19)

Even if all of them believed like Joshua and Caleb, they still would have had to wait the thirteen months so that their entry into the Promised Land would have been a great blessing. The children of Israel had to learn how to follow and trust God, how to be a nation and govern themselves according to God's instructions, and how to live with God in their midst. Additionally, time was needed for the giants to build great cities and good houses, to fill the houses with good things, to dig deep wells and to plant beautiful vineyards and olive trees to be handed over to God's people.

God would not have brought them in too early. God wants us to believe for fast results, but he doesn't take shortcuts. God's desire to bless us is great, but his desire to develop our character is even greater. We will discuss this in more detail in the next chapter.

Only God knows perfect timing for things, but sometimes our answer is delayed because our faith gets contaminated with fear. God told the children of Israel that he had already given them the land and they were to go in and possess the Promised Land as their inheritance. Because of fear, they wandered in the wilderness and it took forty years before any of the children of Israel actually claimed what God said was already theirs.

We keep on knocking and keep on expecting fast results, even though we see nothing happening, because we keep our eyes on the promise instead of our circumstances. We look at what we are going to and not what we are going through.

We trust in God's perfect timing, but it is normal for God to give fast results. Victory is released when we keep our eyes on God and his promise. Even when things look bad, our miracle is just around the corner. Here are some excerpts from 2 Chronicles chapter 20:

> *"It came to pass after this also, that the children of Moab, and the children of Ammon, and with them other beside the Ammonites, came against Jehoshaphat to battle...And Jehoshaphat stood in the congregation of Judah and Jerusalem, in the house of the LORD, before the new court, And said, O LORD God of our fathers, art not thou God in heaven? and rulest not thou over all the kingdoms of the heathen? and in thine hand is there not power and might, so that none is able to withstand thee? Art not thou our God, who didst drive*

out the inhabitants of this land before thy people Israel, and gavest it to the seed of Abraham thy friend for ever?... And now, behold, the children of Ammon and Moab and mount Seir, whom thou wouldest not let Israel invade, when they came out of the land of Egypt, but they turned from them, and destroyed them not; Behold, I say, how they reward us, to come to cast us out of thy possession, which thou hast given us to inherit. O our God, wilt thou not judge them? for we have no might against this great company that cometh against us; neither know we what to do: but our eyes are upon thee. And all Judah stood before the LORD, with their little ones, their wives, and their children. Then upon Jahaziel the son of Zechariah, the son of Benaiah, the son of Jeiel, the son of Mattaniah, a Levite of the sons of Asaph, came the Spirit of the LORD in the midst of the congregation; And he said, Hearken ye, all Judah, and ye inhabitants of Jerusalem, and thou king Jehoshaphat, Thus saith the LORD unto you, Be not afraid nor dismayed by reason of this great multitude; for the battle is not yours, but God's. Tomorrow go ye down against them: behold, they come up by the cliff of Ziz; and ye shall find them at the end of the brook, before the wilderness of Jeruel. Ye shall not need to fight in this battle: set yourselves, stand ye still, and see the salvation of the LORD with you, O Judah and Jerusalem: fear not, nor be dismayed; tomorrow go out against them: for the LORD will be with you...And when they began to sing and to praise, the LORD set ambushments against the children of Ammon, Moab, and mount Seir, which were come against Judah; and they were smitten. For the children of Ammon and Moab stood up against the inhabitants of mount Seir, utterly to slay and destroy them: and when they had made an end of the inhabitants of Seir, every one helped to destroy another. And when Judah came toward the watch tower in the wilderness, they looked unto the multitude, and, behold, they were dead bodies fallen to the earth, and none escaped. And when Jehoshaphat and his people came to take away the spoil of them, they found among them in abundance *both riches with the dead bodies, and precious jewels, which they stripped off for themselves, more than they could carry away: and they were three days in gathering of the spoil, it was so much."* (2 Chronicles 20:1, 5-7, 10-17, 22-25)

God will often lead his people into a fight in which it is impossible for them to win in their own abilities. It is a fight of faith to believe that God has already given us the victory. All of Judah's eyes were on the Lord and his promise, and not on the enemy. They couldn't win any other way. They didn't have the might or power (their own strength) to defeat the enemy, and they didn't know what to do. They simply kept their eyes on the Lord because they knew that the battle was not theirs but God's. They knew that the Father "he doeth the works."

"Then he answered and spake unto me, saying, This is the word of the LORD unto Zerubbabel, saying, Not by might, nor by power, but by my spirit, saith the LORD of hosts." (Zechariah 4:6)

The Spirit of the Lord spoke through Jahaziel saying the battle is the Lord's and to stand still and see the salvation of the Lord, and tomorrow go out against them. He didn't say, let's have a long drawn out battle that will last forty years. Be willing to go forty years if necessary, but be expecting today or tomorrow.

Let's look at more examples showing the swiftness and suddenness in which God operates.

"And Moses said unto the people, Fear ye not, stand still, and see the salvation of the LORD, which he will shew to you today: for the Egyptians whom ye have seen today, ye shall see them again no more forever." (Exodus 14:13)

"Then said David to the Philistine, Thou comest to me with

a sword, and with a spear, and with a shield: but I come to thee in the name of the LORD of hosts, the God of the armies of Israel, whom thou hast defied. This day will the LORD deliver thee into mine hand; and I will smite thee, and take thine head from thee; and I will give the carcases of the host of the Philistines this day unto the fowls of the air, and to the wild beasts of the earth, that all the earth may know that there is a God in Israel." (1 Samuel 17:45-46)

We need to develop our faith for God to deliver us speedily, yet be willing to fight that particular fight all the days of our life, if necessary, all the while looking for the victory each day. There are still giants (natural circumstances that make things difficult or impossible) today and their purpose is to bring fear to stop our faith to receive the promise. We must keep our eyes not only on the promise, but on the One who promises.

"Looking unto Jesus the author and finisher of our faith; who for the joy that was set before him endured the cross, despising the shame, and is set down at the right hand of the throne of God." (Hebrews 12:2)

Notice the timing in the following examples of miracles in the earthly ministry of the Lord Jesus Christ. None of these are duplicated instances.

"And, behold, there came a leper and worshipped him, saying, Lord, if thou wilt, thou canst make me clean. And Jesus put forth his hand, and touched him, saying, I will; be thou clean. And immediately his leprosy was cleansed." (Matthew 8:2-3)

"And Jesus said unto the centurion, Go thy way; and as thou hast believed, so be it done unto thee. And his servant was healed in the selfsame hour." (Matthew 8:13)

"Then Jesus answered and said unto her, O woman, great is thy faith: be it unto thee even as thou wilt. And her daughter was made whole from that very hour." (Matthew 15:28)

"And Jesus rebuked the devil; and he departed out of him: and the child was cured from that very hour." (Matthew 17:18)

"But Simon's wife's mother lay sick of a fever, and anon they tell him of her. And he came and took her by the hand, and lifted her up; and immediately the fever left her, and she ministered unto them." (Matthew 1:30-31)

"I say unto thee, Arise, and take up thy bed, and go thy way into thine house. And immediately he arose, took up the bed, and went forth before them all; insomuch that they were all amazed, and glorified God, saying, We never saw it on this fashion." (Mark 2:11-12)

"For she said, If I may touch but his clothes, I shall be whole. And straightway the fountain of her blood was dried up; and she felt in her body that she was healed of that plague." (Mark 5:28-29)

"And looking up to heaven, he sighed, and saith unto him, Ephphatha, that is, Be opened. And straightway his ears were opened, and the string of his tongue was loosed, and he spake plain." (Mark 7:34-35)

"And all wept, and bewailed her: but he said, Weep not; she is not dead, but sleepeth. And they laughed him to scorn, knowing that she was dead. And he put them all out, and took her by the hand, and called, saying, Maid, arise. And her spirit came again, and she arose straightway: and he commanded to give her meat." (Luke 8:52-55)

"And, behold, there was a woman which had a spirit of

infirmity eighteen years, and was bowed together, and could in no wise lift up herself. And when Jesus saw her, he called her to him, and said unto her, Woman, thou art loosed from thine infirmity. And he laid his hands on her: and immediately she was made straight, and glorified God." (Luke 13:11-13)

"Saying, What wilt thou that I shall do unto thee? And he said, Lord, that I may receive my sight. And Jesus said unto him, Receive thy sight: thy faith hath saved thee. And immediately he received his sight, and followed him, glorifying God: and all the people, when they saw it, gave praise unto God." (Luke 18:41-43)

"The impotent man answered him, Sir, I have no man, when the water is troubled, to put me into the pool: but while I am coming, another steppeth down before me. Jesus saith unto him, Rise, take up thy bed, and walk. And immediately the man was made whole, and took up his bed, and walked: and on the same day was the Sabbath." (John 5:7-9)

"So when they had rowed about five and twenty or thirty furlongs, they see Jesus walking on the sea, and drawing nigh unto the ship: and they were afraid. But he saith unto them, It is I; be not afraid. Then they willingly received him into the ship: and immediately the ship was at the land whither they went." (John 6:19-21)

Some people think it is presumptuous to expect the same results in our ministry that were achieved by Jesus, the Son of God. Jesus said that not only could we receive the same results, but that we could do more.

"Verily, verily, I say unto you, He that believeth on me, the works that I do shall he do also; and greater works than these shall he do; because I go unto my Father. And whatsoever ye shall ask in my name, that will I do, that the Father may be

glorified in the Son. If ye shall ask any thing in my name, I will do it." (John 14:12-14)

"And when he had called unto him his twelve disciples, he gave them power against unclean spirits, to cast them out, and to heal all manner of sickness and all manner of disease." (Matthew 10:1)

David prayed and asked God to answer his prayers speedily. God didn't call him presumptuous, but, rather, called David a man after his own heart. And we have a new and better covenant than David!

"In thee, O LORD, do I put my trust; let me never be ashamed: deliver me in thy righteousness. Bow down thine ear to me; deliver me speedily: be thou my strong rock, for an house of defence to save me For thou art my rock and my fortress; therefore for thy name's sake lead me, and guide me," (Psalm 31:1-3)

"Hear my prayer, O LORD, and let my cry come unto thee. Hide not thy face from me in the day when I am in trouble; incline thine ear unto me: in the day when I call answer me speedily." (Psalm 102:1-2)

"And hide not thy face from thy servant; for I am in trouble: hear me speedily." (Psalm 69:17)

"I stretch forth my hands unto thee: my soul thirsteth after thee, as a thirsty land. Selah. Hear me speedily, O LORD: my spirit faileth: hide not thy face from me, lest I be like unto them that go down into the pit. Cause me to hear thy lovingkindness in the morning; for in thee do I trust: cause me to know the way wherein I should walk; for I lift up my soul unto thee." (Psalm 143:6-8)

> "And afterward they desired a king: and God gave unto them Saul the son of Cis, a man of the tribe of Benjamin, by the space of forty years. And when he had removed him, he raised up unto them David to be their king; to whom also he gave testimony, and said, I have found David the son of Jesse, a man after mine own heart, which shall fulfil all my will" (Acts 13:21-22).

With our new and better covenant, we should not back down from praying and expecting the results like David and Jesus did. Here are some examples of New Testament believers who received immediate answers.

> "Then Peter said, Silver and gold have I none; but such as I have give I thee: In the name of Jesus Christ of Nazareth rise up and walk. And he took him by the right hand, and lifted him up: and immediately his feet and ankle bones received strength." (Acts 3:6-7)

> "And Peter said unto him, Aeneas, Jesus Christ maketh thee whole: arise, and make thy bed. And he arose immediately." (Acts 9:34)

> "And at midnight Paul and Silas prayed, and sang praises unto God: and the prisoners heard them. And suddenly there was a great earthquake, so that the foundations of the prison were shaken: and immediately all the doors were opened, and every one's bands were loosed." (Acts 16:25-26)

God is never early and he is never late. Expect results speedily. Be looking for them immediately. If you must wait, rejoice in the knowledge that God is working in the unseen world to bring about something even better than you were expecting. When one door closes, God is about to open a new door that leads to an even bigger and better victory. It may be that it is taking longer so that spoil can be gathered up. Giants may be digging a deep well for you. Remember, you should keep looking at what you are going to and not what you are going through.

The enemy wants us to have a poverty mentality and to think that every battle will be an exhausting, long, drawn-out one. He wants us to think about an overwhelming ordeal and quit because the battle won't be worth it. The devil is a liar. A victory from God is always worth the fight! Many Christians are experiencing long, arduous battles in their finances, in their health, or in a courtroom, because that is what they are expecting. If you believe for deliverance in the sweet by and by, then that's what you will get. You get what you expect.

"For as he thinketh in his heart, so is he." (Proverbs 23:7)

I want to share with you a personal testimony of praying for a speedy deliverance to avoid a long, drawn-out battle. Several years ago, when I left my last employment in the business world before entering into full time ministry, I was owed a bonus. It was a considerable amount of money. I had a contract that clearly defined the particulars relating to my bonus. There should have been no dispute.

When the deadline passed for the issuance of my check (nine months after my departure), I sent an email of inquiry to my former boss. He responded with a letter stating that there would be no bonus check issued to me. This came from a man who is obsessed with winning, especially court battles. I considered this development as an attempt from the enemy to steal from a child of God.

I visited an attorney the following day and showed him my contract. He put together a letter demanding the payment of my bonus. The letter was sent out for overnight delivery addressed to my former boss. I prayed that God would avenge me of my adversary speedily. Two days later, I received a call from my attorney and after I said hello he started the conversation with these words. "Congratulations, you have just received the fastest settlement in the history of my practice." He had the check in his hand and it was for the full amount.

My attorney received the check the second day after sending the letter. That means that my former boss had to authorize the check to be issued in full and sent for overnight delivery the same day that he received the letter. That's speedy delivery. If I had believed for a victory through a long, drawn-out battle, then that's what would have happened. Most of the amount of my bonus would have been consumed in legal fees leaving very little for me to enjoy. Because I believed for a speedy delivery, I was able to enjoy virtually all of my bonus.

We don't have to wait forty years to walk in the promises of God, and we don't have to wait thirty-eight years to be healed like the man at the pool of Bethesda. God wants us to be delivered speedily! The enemy's strategy is to try to wear us down until we give up or die. He wants to convince us to believe for a long battle so that our victory is deferred.

"Hope deferred maketh the heart sick." (Prov. 13:12)

Though battles are necessary, God never intends for us to stay in them. We walk through the valley of the shadow of death; we don't pitch a tent and camp out there. God has planned for us to win every battle and win them all overwhelmingly and speedily. If we are focused on the promise of God, any delay from God is just to make the victory that much greater, the blessing easier to enjoy, adding spoils to make the victory that much sweeter.

CHAPTER FOUR

GOD TAKES NO SHORTCUTS

Even though God wants to deliver us speedily, he does not take shortcuts with our lives. He always does what is best for us. He directs us to the most good for our lives.

"And the LORD commanded us to do all these statutes, to fear the LORD our God, for our good always, that he might preserve us alive, as it is at this day." (Deuteronomy 6:24)

"How God anointed Jesus of Nazareth with the Holy Ghost and with power: who went about doing good, and healing all that were oppressed of the devil; for God was with him." (Acts 10:38)

"For the LORD God is a sun and shield: the LORD will give grace and glory: no good thing will he withhold from them that walk uprightly. O LORD of hosts, blessed is the man that trusteth in thee." (Psalm 84:11-12)

God will win through love and he won't fail because "love never fails". God will not take you on a short route when a longer route is better for you.

> *"And it came to pass, when Pharaoh had let the people go, that God led them not through the way of the land of the Philistines, although that was near; for God said, Lest peradventure the people repent when they see war, and they return to Egypt."* (Exodus 13: 17).

The shortest, quickest route was through the land of the Philistines. God will use the route that is best for us. It is different for each person in each situation. We earlier discussed that it took about thirteen months to get the children of Israel ready for the Promised Land, even if they would have made the decision to believe God. Remember, though, that the Israelites had hundreds of years of Egypt (the world) programmed into their thinking.

Jesus is our example. We look to him to know how to operate on this earth.

> *"For I have given you an example, that ye should do as I have done to you."* (John 13:15)

> *"Be ye therefore followers of God, as dear children; And walk in love, as Christ also hath loved us, and hath given himself for us an offering and a sacrifice to God for a sweetsmelling savour."* (Ephesians 5:1-2)

> *"Be ye followers of me, even as I also am of Christ."* (1 Corinthians 11:1)

Jesus showed us how to overcome when we are tempted by the enemy to take the short and easy route. God may bring quick deliverance, but he never gives us a short cut that will not give us a complete victory and good character development. Jesus is our example. He was tempted by the devil to bypass the way of faith and obedience to take the short and easy route of the world.

> "For all that is in the world, the lust of the flesh, and the lust of the eyes, and the pride of life, is not of the Father, but is of the world." (1 John 2:16)

All temptations fit into one of those categories listed in 1 John 2:16. Remember, there is a difference between temptation and testing. The devil wants us to walk by sight and not by faith, but God wants us to walk by faith and not by sight. God is not bringing bad things into our lives. God will not make you sick, he will not sow tares and thorns in your life, he will not send storms, and he will not tempt you. For more on this subject please see chapter 7 of my book The Goodness of God.

> "Let no man say when he is tempted, I am tempted of God: for God cannot be tempted with evil, neither tempteth he any man." (James 1: 13)

Again, God doesn't send sickness or storms or sow tares or deliver thorns or tempt us, and we should take dominion over these things in the name of Jesus as we look toward what we are going to in the Lord. Well, does that mean that everything that makes us uncomfortable comes from the devil? No, God won't send bad things, but sometimes for our good he may put us in a place where we are uncomfortable. It will be a place where we must stretch our faith. God won't tempt us to do wrong, but he will test his people and he will do that in only one area.

Because he put the kingdom principle of sowing and reaping in the earth, God has a right to test us in the area of provision. He can do that, for he has allowed us to test him or prove him in that area of our lives.

> "Bring ye all the tithes into the storehouse, that there may be meat in mine house, and prove me now herewith, saith the LORD of hosts, if I will not open you the windows of heaven,

and pour you out a blessing, that there shall not be room enough to receive it." (Malachi 3:10)

God proves us just as we prove him. The greatest example of that was when the children of Israel crossed the wilderness to enter into the Promised Land. They had to be proved first so their faithfulness would enable them to enjoy and be blessed when walking in the land of the promises of God.

"And thou shalt remember all the way which the LORD thy God led thee these forty years in the wilderness, to humble thee, and to prove thee, to know what was in thine heart, whether thou wouldest keep his commandments, or no." (Deuteronomy 8:2)

The trip into the Promised Land would have been a short journey if only they would have passed the test right away. God is a good educator. He won't pass you to the next level unless you pass the test. (Current educators should take a lesson from God.) The most prominent thing that I see in the Israelites period of learning, which should have been very short, is that God doesn't take things away from us in order to teach us.

Notice that God's people had fresh, nourishing food every day. They had fresh water every day, even if it had to come out of a rock. They had fellowship with each other and experienced the presence of God. Their clothes and shoes were like new every day and never wore out, even after forty years. They had protection and guidance with the clouds by day and the pillar of fire by night. They witnessed the supernatural provision of God every day. Not one person ever got sick, not even one. Oh yes, they even had great wealth with a large amount of gold because they took the spoils from the Egyptians. Notice God took none of these things away from them.

He wants us to learn from him willingly because we honor

his word and his voice. The children of Israel did squander much of their gold by forming a golden calf. That was an act of disobedience and certainly not directed by God. If we will obey God and be faithful with our tithes and offerings, then we are proved as we prove God and we can move into our promised land. As long as we are on this earth, we will always have to sow seeds beyond our perceived abilities to go to the next level with God. As we do, God will teach us and we'll experience an increase, not a loss, for God doesn't have to take good things from us to teach us. If God doesn't want us to have something, then we shouldn't want it, because all good things come from God.

"Every good gift and every perfect gift is from above, and cometh down from the Father of lights, with whom is no variableness, neither shadow of turning." (James 1:17)

All the children of Israel had to learn was three things. Before entering the Promised Land, they had to learn that God is the source of all provision. They had to learn that God is a good provider. They had to learn to follow God wherever he leads them, for he always took them to places of provision. We should learn these things too. Anything that comes from God is to bless us. He wants to lead us into a good place. There is no need to be afraid, no matter how things look.

"When thou passest through the waters, I will be with thee; and through the rivers, they shall not overflow thee: when thou walkest through the fire, thou shalt not be burned; neither shall the flame kindle upon thee." (Isaiah 43:2)

"The LORD is my shepherd; I shall not want. He maketh me to lie down in green pastures: he leadeth me beside the still waters." (Psalm 23: 1-2)

If we trust God, we will not be drowned and we will not be burned because Jesus overcame all tribulations for us. The crown of thorns representing tribulations caused blood to flow to bring victory for us. It brought us victory over tribulations because the blood has freed our minds to think about the joy that is set before us rather than what we are going through. That is why we can rejoice in the fiery trial, because promotion is always our reward when we come through the fire.

We cast our cares upon Jesus because he cares for us. We are not made to carry heavy burdens. They can weigh us down and destroy us. We must give them to God and let him handle them. He knows what to do when we don't.

> *"Come unto me, all ye that labour and are heavy laden, and I will give you rest. Take my yoke upon you, and learn of me; for I am meek and lowly in heart: and ye shall find rest unto your souls. For my yoke is easy, and my burden is light."* (Matthew11:28-30)

Promotion always comes when we make it through the fiery trial. We can rejoice because we can make it through. Blessings and promotion are waiting at the end of this short journey!

> *"And these three men, Shadrach, Meshach, and Abed-nego, fell down bound into the midst of the burning fiery furnace. Then Nebuchadnezzar the king was astonied, and rose up in haste, and spake, and said unto his counsellers, Did not we cast three men bound into the midst of the fire? They answered and said unto the king, True, O king. He answered and said, Lo, I see four men loose, walking in the midst of the fire, and they have no hurt; and the form of the fourth is like the Son of God. Then Nebuchadnezzar came near to the mouth of the burning fiery furnace, and spake, and said, Shadrach, Meshach, and Abed-nego, ye servants of the most high God,*

come forth, and come hither. Then Shadrach, Meshach, and Abed-nego, came forth of the midst of the fire. And the princes, governors, and captains, and the king's counsellors, being gathered together, saw these men, upon whose bodies the fire had no power, nor was an hair of their head singed, neither were their coats changed, nor the smell of fire had passed on them. Then Nebuchadnezzar spake, and said, Blessed be the God of Shadrach, Meshach, and Abed-nego, who hath sent his angel, and delivered his servants that trusted in him, and have changed the king's word, and yielded their bodies, that they might not serve nor worship any god, except their own God. Therefore I make a decree, That every people, nation, and language, which speak any thing amiss against the God of Shadrach, Meshach, and Abed-nego, shall be cut in pieces, and their houses shall be made a dunghill: because there is no other God that can deliver after this sort. Then the king promoted Shadrach, Meshach, and Abed-nego, in the province of Babylon." (Daniel 3: 23-30)

We don't have to look at our problems. We keep looking unto Jesus for the joy or promotion set before us. God has designed us to be reward motivated. God does not make mistakes. He designed us that way and knows what he is doing. If it is wrong to be reward motivated, then Jesus was wrong.

"Looking unto Jesus the author and finisher of our faith; who for the joy that was set before him endured the cross, despising the shame, and is set down at the right hand of the throne of God." (Hebrews 12:2)

"But without faith it is impossible to please him: for he that cometh to God must believe that he is, and that he is a rewarder of them that diligently seek him." (Hebrews 11:6)

Jesus was motivated by looking to his reward and

promotion after enduring the cross. We can endure the crucifying of our flesh if we keep looking unto Jesus and his reward of promotion. Jesus endured the most and therefore got the greatest promotion. Our promotion will come for us just like it did for Jesus, but we must know that it is coming and look forward to it. We don't want to go through a fiery trial and then miss our reward. We should be like Jesus and receive our promotion by faith.

> *"Let this mind be in you, which was also in Christ Jesus: Who, being in the form of God, thought it not robbery to be equal with God: But made himself of no reputation, and took upon him the form of a servant, and was made in the likeness of men: And being found in fashion as a man, he humbled himself, and became obedient unto death, even the death of the cross. Wherefore God also hath highly exalted him, and given him a name which is above every name: That at the name of Jesus every knee should bow, of things in heaven, and things in earth, and things under the earth; And that every tongue should confess that Jesus Christ is Lord, to the glory of God the Father."* (Philippians 2: 5-11)

Jesus is our example. He showed us how and has empowered us to overcome the temptation to take the route that the world takes. The enemy will appeal to our natural mind, thus making the route of the world's way look faster and better. The devil is a liar. We take the path of obedience as instructed by our heavenly Father. His way will never violate kingdom principles.

Jesus overcame temptation from the enemy, not as God but as a man, thus showing the way for our victory over temptation. Let's see how Jesus overcame the same temptations that the devil used to tempt Adam and Eve. Let's compare the responses.

> *"And Jesus being full of the Holy Ghost returned from*

Jordan, and was led by the Spirit into the wilderness, Being forty days tempted of the devil. And in those days he did eat nothing: and when they were ended, he afterward hungered." (Luke 4:1-2)

Notice that Jesus was led by the Spirit to be tempted. We are not led by the Spirit to be tempted, because God does not tempt any man as we read in James 1:13 above. Jesus had to be tempted and win the victory so we could have the victory over temptation. Jesus became sick so we could be healed. He became poor so that through his poverty we might be made rich. Jesus was made sin so we could be made righteous. He was forsaken so we could never be forsaken. He was punished for our sin so that we could receive the grace of God. He was led to be tempted so that we are not led into temptation but delivered from evil.

Jesus showed us how to overcome temptation as a man. After forty days of fasting, Jesus was hungry. He wanted bread. His natural body of a man wanted food and he was tempted. This was a temptation of the lust of the flesh.

"And the devil said unto him, If thou be the Son of God, command this stone that it be made bread." (Luke 4:3)

Let's look at Genesis 3:6.

"And when the woman saw that the tree was good for food, and that it was pleasant to the eyes, and a tree to be desired to make one wise, she took of the fruit thereof, and did eat, and gave also unto her husband with her; and he did eat." (Genesis 3:6)

The tree was good for food. The devil tells her to eat it. She gives in and so does her husband. They gave in to the temptation of the lust of the flesh with their disobedient response toward God's instructions. Let's look at the response of Jesus to the lust of the flesh.

> "And Jesus answered him, saying, It is written, That man shall not live by bread alone, but by every word of God." (Luke 4:4)

Jesus responds with the Word of God and quotes Deuteronomy 8:3. Notice that the devil was tempting Jesus the whole time of the fast as shown in Luke 2:2: "Being forty days tempted of the devil." He gave the strongest temptation when Jesus was at his weakest. When we are going good and winning, the devil usually stays back and lets our pride bring us down. He lets us get a glimpse of ourselves on top and hopes we will be like the character Richard Castle on the television series Castle. We get a glimpse of a reflection of ourselves and we say, "I really am ruggedly handsome."

Jesus was hungry, but the Father wanted us to get victory over temptation and therefore sustained Jesus through his forty-day fast. Jesus knew the purpose and rejected the evil offer of Satan. The offer was to use his position as the Son of God as authority to satisfy hunger rather than relying on God's purpose and provision as Israel had been taught. In other words, overcome as God rather than as a man who relies totally on his heavenly Father. During the period of the fast, Jesus was living by God's Word, living out Deuteronomy 8:3, demonstrating that man shall not live by bread alone.

The lust of the flesh was followed by the temptation of the lust of the eyes for Adam and Jesus, the last Adam. Adam was tempted as the tree was pleasant to the eyes according to Genesis 3:6. Jesus was likewise tempted.

> "And the devil, taking him up into an high mountain, shewed unto him all the kingdoms of the world in a moment of time. And the devil said unto him, All this power will I give thee, and the glory of them: for that is delivered unto me; and

> to whomsoever I will I give it. If thou therefore wilt worship me, all shall be thine." (Luke 4:5-7)

We know Adam and Eve's response. Let's see the response of Jesus.

> "And Jesus answered and said unto him, Get thee behind me, Satan: for it is written, Thou shalt worship the Lord thy God, and him only shalt thou serve." (Luke 4:8)

Jesus answered with the Word of God quoting Deuteronomy 6:13. Satan had the world at that time, because Adam had defaulted. Jesus, as the last Adam, was about to take it back. He was going to do it the Father's way, the way of the cross, not the shortcut way of the land of the Philistines.

What the devil was saying to Jesus was that if he was the Son of God he didn't need the cross to take back the world. Jesus went to the cross because the Father wanted to give this earth back to men, and the cross was the only way. Jesus obeyed the Father.

> "The heaven, even the heavens, are the LORD's: but the earth hath he given to the children of men." (Psalm 115:16)

> "Philip saith unto him, Lord, shew us the Father, and it sufficeth us. Jesus saith unto him, Have I been so long time with you, and yet hast thou not known me, Philip? he that hath seen me hath seen the Father; and how sayest thou then, Shew us the Father? Believest thou not that I am in the Father, and the Father in me? the words that I speak unto you I speak not of myself: but the Father that dwelleth in me, he doeth the works." (John 14:8-10)

Jesus only did what the Father told him to do and he only said what the Father told him to say. He didn't do his own will. He just did the will of the Father. The Father's will is to give the earth to men. God said let us make man but let them have dominion.

Jesus was exalted by his Father because of his obedience and because he put on the form of a servant. He was not exalted because he was a big shot. It's the same for you and me. As our example, Jesus had to go by way of the cross. Now we pick up our cross and follow him. A cross is a place where flesh is crucified and there is total dependence upon the Father.

The devil next tempted Jesus, just as he did Adam and Eve, with the pride of life. As we can see in Genesis 3:6, eating from the tree of life was "desired to make one wise." Adam and Eve's response was disobedience that resulted in guilt and shame. Jesus, however, had an altogether different response. His response was in obedience to his Father, even though he was tempted with the pride of life.

> "And he brought him to Jerusalem, and set him on a pinnacle of the temple, and said unto him, If thou be the Son of God, cast thyself down from hence: For it is written, He shall give his angels charge over thee, to keep thee: And in their hands they shall bear thee up, lest at any time thou dash thy foot against a stone." (Luke 4:9-11)

The devil was quoting Psalm 91:11-12, but he added something and left something out. This is a clever trick he still uses today. He added "at any time" and he left out "in all thy ways." Let's see the response of Jesus.

> "And Jesus answering said unto him, It is said, Thou shalt not tempt the Lord thy God." (Luke 4:12)

Jesus quoted Deuteronomy 6:16. Satan used his quote out of context, used it incorrectly, and even added something. Jesus put him in his place right away. Jesus knew the Scriptures because he was, he is, and will always be the Logos, the Word of God.

"In the beginning was the Word, and the Word was with God, and the Word was God. The same was in the beginning with God. All things were made by him; and without him was not anything made that was made. In him was life; and the life was the light of men." (John 1:1-4)

"Ye shall not add unto the word which I command you, neither shall ye diminish ought from it, that ye may keep the commandments of the LORD your God which I command you." (Deut. 4:2)

Jesus said in Matthew 22:29 that we "do err, not knowing the scriptures." The more Word we have in us the less likely we are to err or to yield to temptation. The temptation of the stones into bread (lust of the flesh) and the temptation of casting down from the highest point of the temple (pride of life) both address unbelief, the lack of confidence in God's provision and his faithfulness.

The other temptation concerned God's primary prohibition to Israel, namely, the worship of other gods (lust of the eyes). Jesus responded angrily in Luke 4:8 saying, "get thee behind me Satan." Jesus responded with anger but sinned not, for God is a jealous God. He is jealous for our love. He is not jealous like men and women get jealous. There is a different Hebrew word to describe God's jealousy as opposed to man's sin of jealousy. God is merely protective of what belongs to him. There is a godly jealousy. The apostle Paul had godly jealousy for the church at Corinth.

"For I am jealous over you with godly jealousy: for I have espoused you to one husband, that I may present you as a chaste virgin to Christ. But I fear, lest by any means, as the serpent beguiled Eve through his subtilty, so your minds should be corrupted from the simplicity that is in Christ." (2 Cor. 11:2-3)

There is a "marriage ceremony" between Israel and God and between the redeemed and God. A Jew or Christian who engages in idolatry is like a spouse who willfully engages in adultery, for indeed, idolatry is a form of spiritual adultery. The Lord watches over Israel and the redeemed lovingly and closely, like a faithful and passionate husband watches over his beloved wife.

The devil tempted Jesus with the ability to rule the world. Jesus would eventually have that, but it had to come in obedience to the Father and thus by way of the cross. As we are in Christ, those born again can rule the world as Jesus has given us dominion over the things of this world. The exercise of this authority and dominion is also manifested through obedience. We will likewise be tempted as Jesus was. This temptation from the devil makes me think of what Jesus said about such temptations to us.

> *"For what is a man profited, if he shall gain the whole world, and lose his own soul? or what shall a man give in exchange for his soul?"* (Matt. 16:26)

Jesus received exactly that proposition. It was a proposition of a shortcut to the kingdom, a way around the cross and he turned it down. He was tempted and he was obedient to God's plan and God's purpose.

> *"Because he himself suffered when he was tempted, he is able to help those who are being tempted."* (Hebrews 2:18 NIV)

> *"For we have not an high priest which cannot be touched with the feeling of our infirmities; but was in all points tempted like as we are, yet without sin. Let us therefore come boldly unto the throne of grace, that we may obtain mercy, and find grace to help in time of need."* (Hebrews 4:15-16)

Through his suffering and decision for obedience, Jesus

has made the way for us to be obedient, even when we are tempted, by overcoming temptation through the Word and the promises of God. No wonder the Father said the following about Jesus:

> "And Jesus, when he was baptized, went up straightway out of the water: and, lo, the heavens were opened unto him, and he saw the Spirit of God descending like a dove, and lighting upon him: And lo a voice from heaven, saying, This is my beloved Son, in whom I am well pleased." (Matthew 3:16-17)

CHAPTER FIVE

JESUS—BEEN THERE, DONE THAT

As we have already discussed, there is no trial that you could go through that Jesus hasn't already made a way of victory. He knows exactly what you are feeling as you go through it. Jesus has been there, done that, and got the T-shirt.

We will definitely feel the oppression as we switch systems from the world's Babylonian system of darkness to the system of the Kingdom of God. As we are transformed by the renewing of our minds, we will confront the world's philosophies. This will cause conflicts, causing us to leave our comfort zones and bring about persecutions.

To be successful at switching systems, we must know what God's will is for us. We must know that God is always for us and never against us. It's time to stop asking why God allows bad things and start asking why we (the body of Christ) allow bad things as Jesus has given his church dominion over the things of this world, including the world system.

We have to change our thinking. Many people today, and even most preachers, think that everything that happens on the earth is caused by God and that he approves everything before it can happen. If that's true, then God has not truly given us a free will.

We were given dominion over the things of this world. God established man's dominion from the very moment he created us.

> "And God said, Let us make man in our image, after our likeness: and let them have dominion over the fish of the sea, and over the fowl of the air, and over the cattle, and over all the earth, and over every creeping thing that creepeth upon the earth. So God created man in his own image, in the image of God created he him; male and female created he them. And God blessed them, and God said unto them, Be fruitful, and multiply, and replenish the earth, and subdue it: and have dominion over the fish of the sea, and over the fowl of the air, and over every living thing that moveth upon the earth." (Genesis 1:26-28)

Notice how God said, "Let us make man" but "let them have dominion." God is not to take dominion over the affairs of the earth because he gave that task to you and me.

> "The heaven, even the heavens, are the LORD's: but the earth hath he given to the children of men," (Psalm 115:16)

We are to use our free will to freely live under God's authority as ambassadors to earth and do the will of the Father just like Jesus did. We take dominion because God has given us the authority to do it. We are made in the likeness of God to function like God on this earth.

> "Now then we are ambassadors for Christ, as though God did beseech you by us: we pray you in Christ's stead, be ye reconciled to God." (2 Corinthians 5:20)

An ambassador is supposed to do the will of the country or kingdom he represents. If I am a good ambassador, I don't do what I think is best, but I do the will of and represent the one who sent me. Jesus was the perfect example.

Man lost his dominion through sin, but Jesus came and restored back to us everything that Adam had lost.

> "Therefore as by the offence of the judgement came upon all men to condemnation: even so by the righteousness of one free gift upon all men unto justification of life. For as by one man's disobedience many were made sinners, so by the obedience of one shall many be made righteous." (Romans 5:18-19)

To change things on the earth, Jesus, the second and last Adam, had to come to earth as a man because God gave dominion in the earth to man, not to himself. Jesus, as a sinless man, has put us back in the same place of dominion that Adam and Eve had before sin entered the earth. The difference for us now is that we have to deal with the effects of sin, as it is still prevalent on the earth. This means that all the more we must take dominion over the systems of this world, giving the system of the Kingdom of God a place of dominance.

Man is a spiritual being like our God is. Yet, man was also meant to rule in the physical realm. Therefore, God gave physical bodies to mankind. Jesus came as God in the physical body of a man to set things in order on the earth. To loose his power on the earth, God always uses a man, woman, boy, or girl in a human body, because God has said, "Let them have dominion." God does not stray from what he declares.

> "God is not a man, that he should lie; neither the son of a man, that he should repent: hath he said, and shall he not do it? or hath he spoken, and shall he not make it good?" (Numbers 23:19)

God is legally bound to work through willing people, and he is not a lawless one like Satan. We are the ones who have to cooperate with God to make good things on earth as they are in heaven. Without God, we cannot, but without us, God will not. People believe that everything that happens is God's will. Really? Every murder, sickness, rape, and child molestation is God's will? That is so far from the truth. If God controls everything then we shouldn't prosecute a child molester because, after all, God was in control. We shouldn't pray to be healed because God is in control. There is no sickness in God and he can't give you what he doesn't have.

Not everything that happens in this earth is God's will. God's will is like it is in heaven. He wants to use you and me to bring his will on earth as it is in heaven. The Bible says that God does not want anyone to perish, yet we know that people die and go to hell every day. Therefore, his will is not always done on earth.

> *"The Lord is not slack concerning his promise, as some men count slackness; but is longsuffering to us-ward, not willing that any should perish, but that all should come to repentance."* (2 Peter 3:9)

If we want to see God's will of blessing in people's lives because they repent, simply tell them of the goodness of God. Telling them that they have messed up won't accomplish much, because people already know that. The thing that produces the most fruit is to tell them of the goodness of God.

> *"Or depiseth thou the riches of his goodness and forbearance and longsuffering: not knowing that the goodness of God leadeth thee to repentence?"* (Romans 2:4)

God has given us a free will and he lets us use it. God

was not taken by surprise when Adam was about to take a bite of the fruit from the tree of the knowledge of good and evil. God was not caught napping. God knew the horrible and long-lasting devastation to man that would result from this sin. Yet God allowed Adam to eat because he had given Adam a free will. God did not reach down and knock the fruit out of Adam's hand. God is in control of your life only if you let him be in control.

What about tribulations that happen to good people who are yielded to God? Know that those that trust in the Lord will not be ashamed. If we will trust God, he will turn even tribulations to our good. For more on tribulations, please refer to my book The Goodness of God.

> *"For we know all things work together for good to them that love God, to them that are called according to his purpose."* (Romans 8:28)

Each one of us makes the choice to put God in control because we trust him, or to control our own life. God lets us choose.

> *"And if it seems evil unto you to serve the LORD, choose you this day whom you will serve; whether the gods which your fathers served that were on the other side of the flood, or the gods of the Amorites, in whose land ye dwell: but as for me and my house, we will serve the LORD."* (Joshua 24:15)

God works with faithful men and women to bring about change on this earth. The people of God have dominion, and it's up to us to make it on earth as it is in heaven. It's time to quit blaming government and the ungodly for the problems in our nation. God says it's up to his people to bring healing and peace.

> *"If my people, which are called by my name, shall humble*

themselves, and pray, and seek my face, and turn from there wicked ways; then will I hear from heaven, and will forgive their sin, and will heal their land." (2 Chronicles 7:14)

God has given man authority on the earth. He will not intervene on earth without the cooperation of a human clothed in flesh.

"Thus saith the LORD, the Holy One of Israel, and his Maker, Ask me of things to come concerning my sons, and concerning the works of my hands command ye me." (Isaiah 45: 11)

Do we command God? No, but when we command a thing in obedience to him, it is God who performs it. We do not beg God to do things. Instead, we command them to be done as God commanded us to do. Since we can't do it and God won't do it without us, we are, in effect, commanding the works of his hands.

"For verily I say unto you, That whosoever shall say unto this mountain, Be thou removed, and be thou cast into the sea; and shall not doubt in his heart, but shall believe that those things which he saith shall come to pass; he shall have whatsoever he saith." (Mark 11:23)

Even though God has chosen to work with man and has given man dominion over this earth, we can be assured that God's overall plan and the things he has spoken will come to pass on the earth. God will always find someone who will yield to him. After all, it only takes one man for God to move. If we move, God will be with us. When we neglect to pray or to obey God, we are forfeiting the manifested realization of our dominion and authority.

"Yet ye have not, because ye ask not." (James 4:2)

You see, we choose the harvest that we receive.

> "Be not deceived; God is not mocked: for whatsoever a man soweth, that shall he also reap." (Galatians 6:7)

When we walk our own way, we allow God's purposes on the earth to be hindered or delayed. It is awesome to think that the God of the universe trusts you and me to get his work done.

> "I will give unto thee the keys of the kingdom of heaven: and whatsoever thou shalt bind on earth shall be bound in heaven: and whatsoever thou shalt loose on earth shalt be loosed in heaven." (Matthew 16:19)

God's people are equipped to walk and talk like God on the earth as we "calleth those things that be not as though they were" (Romans. 4:17).

Since we are made in the image of God, we have creative power when we believe in our hearts and speak with our mouths. Since dominion was given to man, God uses obedient people to speak on the earth.

> "Surely the LORD God will do nothing, but he revealeth his secret unto his servants the prophets." (Amos 3:7)

The devil needs people to accomplish his will on the earth as well. He cannot accomplish anything without man because Jesus won the victory for us and took back the authority for man.

> "And you, being dead in your sins and the uncircumcision of your flesh, hath he quickened together with him, having forgiven you all trespasses; Blotting out the handwriting of ordinances that was against us, which was contrary to us, and took it out of the way, nailing it to his cross; And having

spoiled principalities and powers, he made a shew of them openly, triumphing over them in it." (Colossians 2:13-15)

The devil oppresses people made in the image of God, so they speak into existence what he wants so he can kill, steal, and destroy. God blesses people made in the image of God so they can speak into existence what he wants so he can bring life, gifts, and restoration.

The battleground is the mind. That's why God has said that we should keep our minds "stayed upon the Lord" so that we can have perfect peace. We should think and meditate on the goodness of God.

"Finally, brethren, whatsoever things are true, whatsoever things are honest, whatsoever things are just, whatsoever things are pure, whatsoever things are lovely, whatsoever things are of good report; if there be any virtue, and if there be any praise, think on these things." (Philippians 4:8)

Our minds should be renewed on the Word of God if we want the blessings of God. What we think and therefore do has a great impact on our life. God has said to ask him of things to come. Que sera, sera (whatever will be will be) has no place in the Kingdom of God. What will be is what we say it will be.

"Thou shalt also decree a thing, and it shall be established unto thee: and the light shall shine upon thy ways." (Job 22:28)

The reason Jesus, our high priest, is touched with the feelings of our infirmities is because all the punishment for sin for all people of all times came upon Jesus on the cross. Whatever malady, trial, tribulation, or issue you may go through, Jesus knows exactly how you feel because it actually came on him.

> "He is despised and rejected of men; a man of sorrows, and acquainted with grief: and we hid as it were our faces from him; he was despised, and we esteemed him not. Surely he hath borne our griefs, and carried our sorrows: yet we did esteem him stricken, smitten of God, and afflicted. But he was wounded for our transgressions, he was bruised for our iniquities: the chastisement of our peace was upon him; and with his stripes we are healed. All we like sheep have gone astray; we have turned every one to his own way; and the LORD hath laid on him the iniquity of us all. He was oppressed, and he was afflicted, yet he opened not his mouth: he is brought as a lamb to the slaughter, and as a sheep before her shearers is dumb, so he openeth not his mouth." (Isaiah 53:3-7).

God does not afflict his children. He may require that we leave our comfort zone and stretch our faith but he will not afflict his children. Doesn't it hurt you more when your children are hurt than if you are hurt? If God were to afflict his people he would be afflicting himself. We are not afflicted of God because Jesus took the afflictions that we deserve. He was stricken of God and afflicted.

> "Touching the Almighty, we cannot find him out: he is excellent in power, and in judgment, and in plenty of justice: he will not afflict." (Job 37:23)

> "I will mention the lovingkindnesses of the LORD, and the praises of the LORD, according to all that the LORD hath bestowed on us, and the great goodness toward the house of Israel, which he hath bestowed on them according to his mercies, and according to the multitude of his lovingkindnesses. For he said, Surely they are my people, children that will not lie: so he was their Saviour. In all their affliction he was afflicted, and the angel of his presence saved them: in his love and in his pity he redeemed them; and he bare them, and carried them all the days of old." (Isaiah 63:7-9)

Jesus is the head and we are his body. If even the smallest part of your body is hurting, the head knows it. Recall the last time you hit your little toe on a table leg. Your head is concerned and all you think about is to stop the hurting. Your head says to your hand, "rub that toe." He is afflicted when we are afflicted because he is mindful that we are dust. He is mindful that we are dust because he is touched with the feelings of our infirmities or, in other words, he feels what we feel.

> *"The LORD is merciful and gracious, slow to anger, and plenteous in mercy. He will not always chide: neither will he keep his anger for ever. He hath not dealt with us after our sins; nor rewarded us according to our iniquities. For as the heaven is high above the earth, so great is his mercy toward them that fear him. As far as the east is from the west, so far hath he removed our transgressions from us. Like as a father pitieth his children, so the LORD pitieth them that fear him. For he knoweth our frame; he remembereth that we are dust."* (Psalm 103:8-14)

> *"Seeing then that we have a great high priest, that is passed into the heavens, Jesus the Son of God, let us hold fast our profession. For we have not an high priest which cannot be touched with the feeling of our infirmities; but was in all points tempted like as we are, yet without sin."* (Hebrews 4:14-16)

Many years ago, I heard a preacher give a testimony about how his mother was treated in the hospital following her surgery. Her doctor had left instructions on the patient's chart instructing the nurse on call to make sure the patient (the preacher's mother) got out of bed and walked twice during the first day. He said he watched as the day shift nurse impatiently prodded his mother along even though the effort was causing his mother great pain. "Come on, the doctor said that you had to walk" she scolded as the patient hesitated due to severe discomfort. The preacher remarked that by the time that his mother was put back in bed, he was sure his mother was not stronger from walking but much weaker and much more fragile.

He bristled as he gathered his thoughts to relay the story. As he continued his account of the episode, his countenance began to brighten as he referred to the nurse working the night shift. He shared how the new nurse handled the walking assignment much differently. "She was so gentle," he mused. He relayed how the different methodology produced an entirely different outcome. This time, upon completion of the short journey, his mother seemed stronger than before and displayed a heightened confidence concerning the length of her recovery period. The new nurse took more time with his mother, especially in getting her out of the bed, which was the most painful part. The caring nurse broke the exercise into smaller increments with short rests between each movement.

Later that evening, the preacher thanked the night shift nurse for her gentleness and asked her why she took so much time and care with his mother to accomplish the walk as instructed by the doctor. "Oh! I've had that same surgery and I know how it feels the first few times you have to get up and walk," she replied.

The same is true for Jesus. Whatever affliction you may go through, he has already taken it on and won the victory. He knows how you feel and he is careful to bring you through as gently as he can. He will know about hurts and disappointments that no one else may see or even know about, because all of them came upon him at the cross.

Yes, Jesus and the Father are one. Your heavenly Father sees things and knows things that no one else knows about. I've got good news. He wants to manifest the victory in your life that Jesus has already won for you.

> "Fear not, little flock; for it is your Father's good pleasure to give you the kingdom." (Luke 12:32)

Remember, the manifestation of the promises of God do not just automatically happen. As "we calleth those things which be not as though they were" provision moves from the unseen world to the seen, natural, three-dimensional world.

Let me share a couple of real life natural stories that illustrate the supernatural story of how our heavenly Father deals with his children. When my son Daniel played his first year of T-ball baseball, he was around the age of five. During his very first game, his team was first up to bat. My son Daniel was placed fourth in the batting order. The first three batters all reached base safely to the delight of family and friends.

It was the left-handed batting Daniel's turn to hit the ball off the tee. He whacked the ball hard and sent a line drive about three feet off the ground and approximately one foot to the second baseman's left. The second sacker closed his eyes in fear, then reached out with his glove. The ball stuck to it as if the ball and glove were lined with Velcro.

Hurray! was reprised as it seemed that everyone celebrated the play. Everyone did celebrate the nice play by such a youngster. Everyone, that is, except my son Daniel. No one else at the park that day noticed any sign of emotion on my son's face. The only person who knew that he was hurting was his daddy. Why? Earthly fathers know when their children are hurting, even if no one else can see it.

This was his first game. He was the first one to make an out. Perhaps he didn't anticipate the possibility of making an out, especially after the first three batters reached base safely. As his daddy, I could see things that no one else could see and I had a great desire to do something for him.

> "If ye then, being evil, know how to give good gifts unto your children, how much more shall your Father which is in heaven give good things to them that ask him?" (Matthew 7:11)

Why would I share such an insignificant event? You might correctly reason that such an event had no consequence at all in his life. The hurt was over as soon as he reached base his next at bat. Even though that is true, it was still important to me, because I am his father.

Doesn't the same thing happen to you and me on a regular basis? We get disappointed because something doesn't turn out like we hoped it would. God, who is the Alpha and the Omega and sees the beginning from the end, knows that an event that disappoints us has no real consequence in our life. He will even take it and turn it to our good.

Even as great as the knowledge and the power of God is, even greater is his love for his children. When we hurt, he hurts. When we are afflicted, he is afflicted. He wants to bring you out of that situation into a place of victory as he helps you develop godly character. God will also use that situation to help teach you new truths that you never understood before.

If we obey him completely, we can learn without heartache. Let me tell you how I taught my son to handle his money. Because he completely obeyed his father, he learned without getting hurt. Moreover, he received a blessing. I can't remember how old he was, but he was at the age to begin to work for the money we gave him and save some of it for things he wanted to buy.

His mother and I explained to him the value of saving money, especially if there was something that he wanted to buy. We also showed him how to shop for the best price. We spent time with him explaining methods helpful in the natural as well as God's kingdom principles, especially the law of sowing and reaping with increase. We not only talked about these things, we tried to demonstrate them through how we lived our lives in front of our children.

Our son followed our teachings to the best of his ability, and it was evident that he really wanted to please his father. He decided that he wanted to buy the newly issued

NFL football video game. He started to save his money in order to make the purchase with his own money. When he felt that he had sufficient funds, he shopped around to find the best price. He found an advertisement for the game at our local Best Buy store that was definitely the best price.

He let me know that he was ready. The next day he gathered the money he thought he would need and I drove him to Best Buy. He found the game he wanted and he took it up to the checkout line. The man behind the counter told him a too high, incorrect price and my son very boldly showed him the ad that he brought with him. "Good shopper," the clerk responded. The clerk then rang up the correct sales price that included sales tax.

I suddenly realized that I hadn't told him about allowing for sales tax. He had done everything right based on what he had learned from his father. Even though he had done his best to please his father, he still came up short. He had done something right that each of us could learn from. While he endeavored to complete a transaction in obedience to his father, he had his father with him just in case something went wrong.

Sometimes even though we have obeyed God as best we can, we can still come up short through lack of knowledge and many other reasons. If you invite your heavenly Father with you wherever you go, he will always make up your lack and then some. That's what happened to my son Daniel.

I was so proud of the way he listened to his parents and of his desire to please his father that I not only paid his sales tax, I bought him another game, paid with cash and let him keep the change. There are great benefits to taking your heavenly Father with you in case you come up short. My son got a lot more than what he thought he would receive from his daddy. If an earthly father would put in extra, how much more would our heavenly Father give us more than we expect.

> "And to know the love of Christ, which passeth knowledge, that ye might be filled with all the fulness of God. Now unto him that is able to do exceeding abundantly above all that we ask or think, according to the power that worketh in us." (Ephesians 3:19-20)

We should always put ourselves in the hands of God. He won't afflict us. He won't bring evil to us or tempt us. He will discipline us because he loves us and wants to develop godly character in us. He will do it with love for our good. It is far better to be disciplined by a loving father than take a beating from the world.

> "If ye endure chastening, God dealeth with you as with sons; for what son is he whom the father chasteneth not? But if ye be without chastisement, whereof all are partakers, then are ye bastards, and not sons. Furthermore we have had fathers of our flesh which corrected us, and we gave them reverence: shall we not much rather be in subjection unto the Father of spirits, and live? For they verily for a few days chastened us after their own pleasure; but he for our profit, that we might be partakers of his holiness. Now no chastening for the present seemeth to be joyous, but grievous: nevertheless afterward it yieldeth the peaceable fruit of righteousness unto them which are exercised thereby." (Hebrews 12:7-11).

Always run to God and never run from God. Remember, Jesus knows how you feel. When you hurt, he hurts. He knows what you're going through and he wants to deliver you. Remember that the deliverance doesn't automatically happen. Because you have a free will, he is waiting for you to come to him, believe and speak his promise, and call things that are not as though they are. Then he will make things on earth as they are in heaven in whatever situation you have put in his hands.

Always take your heavenly Father with you in every

endeavor, because he is always for you and never against you.

> "This then is the message which we have heard of him, and declare unto you, that God is light, and in him is no darkness at all," (1 John 1:5)

CHAPTER SIX

EXPECTING TO RECEIVE

We mentioned earlier in chapter 2 that sometimes we don't recognize our answer from God because we are expecting it in a certain way. We should simply expect God to be faithful and leave it to God as to how he wants to do it. Let's face it. He is smarter than we are. His way is always better than what we expect.

Some people miss out because they aren't expecting anything. They sow a seed, then they turn their back on the harvest. The world system is based on taking from others to gain increase. The system of the Kingdom of God is based on giving to others and then you are increased. We must expect to receive when we give. We always get what we expect. What we believe is where we end up.

"For as he thinketh in his heart, so is he." (Proverbs 23:7)

God wants his people to know that he is for them and not against them. God loves you and is interested in you and cares about what you care about. Those who love God are interested in what he is interested in and what he cares about. What does God care about? He cares about reaching the lost (those not in covenant with him) and he cares about his beloved (those in covenant with him). He wants everyone to be born again and to be part of his beloved.

> *"Beloved, I wish above all things that thou mayest prosper and be in health, even as thy soul prospereth." (3 John 2)*

> *"And he said unto them, Go ye into all the world, and preach the gospel to every creature." (Mark 16:15)*

> *"What man of you, having an hundred sheep, if he lose one of them, doth not leave the ninety and nine in the wilderness, and go after that which is lost, until he find it? And when he hath found it, he layeth it on his shoulders, rejoicing." (Luke 15:4-5)*

> *"But the father said to his servants, Bring forth the best robe, and put it on him; and put a ring on his hand, and shoes on his feet: And bring hither the fatted calf, and kill it; and let us eat, and be merry: For this my son was dead, and is alive again; he was lost, and is found. And they began to be merry." (Luke 15:22-24)*

God wants his beloved to prosper and be in health, not only because he loves us, but because we are the ones who will be faithful and invest in the Kingdom of God. I have found that I can do more for the Kingdom of God with my health and resources than I can if I'm sick and broke.

God wants prosperity in the hands of those who care about his work and his interests, so we can do something about what he is concerned about, namely, reaching the lost and healing his beloved. To accomplish this, God gives his people power to gain wealth to establish his covenant. The covenant is accomplished through the giving principle and as we obey him in giving, God's reward system kicks in.

> "But thou shalt remember the LORD thy God: for it is he that giveth thee power to get wealth, that he may establish his covenant which he sware unto thy fathers, as it is this day." (Deuteronomy 8:18)

> "But this I say, He which soweth sparingly shall reap also sparingly; and he which soweth bountifully shall reap also bountifully. Every man according as he purposeth in his heart, so let him give; not grudgingly, or of necessity: for God loveth a cheerful giver." (1 Corinthians 9:6-7)

We have to first be blessed to be a blessing. We need to get into the right mentality in order to walk in the fullness of the blessings of God. To get in the right mentality, we need to learn to expect to receive when we give. We can accomplish this by studying the parable of the unjust steward in Luke chapter 16.

> "And he said also unto his disciples, There was a certain rich man, which had a steward; and the same was accused unto him that he had wasted his goods. And he called him, and said unto him, How is it that I hear this of thee? give an account of thy stewardship; for thou mayest be no longer steward. Then the steward said within himself, What shall I do? for my lord taketh away from me the stewardship: I cannot dig; to beg I am ashamed. I am resolved what to do, that, when I am put out of the stewardship, they may receive me into their houses. So he called every one of his lord's debtors unto him, and said unto the first, How much owest thou unto my lord? And he said, An hundred measures of oil. And he said unto him, Take thy bill, and sit down quickly, and write fifty. Then said he to another, And how much owest thou? And he said, An hundred measures of wheat. And he said unto him, Take thy bill, and write fourscore. And the lord commended the unjust steward, because he had done wisely: for the children of this world are in their

generation wiser than the children of light." (Luke 16:1-8)

The unjust steward was resolved what to do. He gave away what belonged to the rich man so that when (not if, but when) he's put out of the stewardship, he would be received into one of the rich man's debtors' houses. He wanted a place to go when he got fired.

He definitely gave to get. He gave expecting to receive. Based on our natural mind, we think that verse 8 should say: "you gave away a lot of my money just so you'd have a place to go, and because of that you are fired!" Yet, the rich man doesn't say that. In fact, the rich man commends the unjust steward.

"And the lord commended the unjust steward, because he had done wisely: for the children of this world are in their generation wiser than the children of light." (Luke 16:8)

The steward knew a principle. He knew that what he gave away would come back to him to secure his personal future. The rich man also knew this principle. The rich man had a lot of wisdom. That's why he was so rich. He was pleased with the steward because he had learned how to be a success in life and bless the rich man in the process. That's the kind of steward he wanted.

Apparently, he not only kept the steward on the job, but probably gave him a raise. The rich man was pleased with the steward and said that he had done wisely. If he is wiser, he is worth more money.

Why would Jesus say that the children of this world are wiser than the children of light? In other words, he is saying that in that generation, the world understood giving to get better than his people did. They understood the concept of "you scratch my back and I'll scratch your back." They understood "let's work together" even if they used this principle for evil means, such as building the tower of Babel.

In this current generation that will lead to God's end-time wealth transfer, God's people will surpass the world in the use of this powerful kingdom principle of giving in order to receive.

The steward gave while expecting to receive. Jesus told his disciples that not only did the rich man commend the steward, he also commends him saying that he had done wisely. Why is he wise? He is wise because he gave believing that when he gave, it was going to come back to him and salvage his future. He trusted upon the giving principle to salvage his future when he lost the permanent security of his job.

Who is the rich man in this parable, the one who let the steward know that he would be called to account for his stewardship, and thus caused the steward to lose his permanent security in his job? Let's look at verses 1 and 2 again.

> "And he said also unto his disciples, There was a certain rich man, which had a steward; and the same was accused unto him that he had wasted his goods. And he called him, and said unto him, How is it that I hear this of thee? give an account of thy stewardship; for thou mayest be no longer steward." (Luke 16:1-2)

God is the rich man and Adam is the steward. Adam was God's steward over the earth. God and Adam visited and fellowshipped every day, and Adam gave an account of himself. The earth belonged to God, but Adam was in charge of it. Even after Adam messed up, God came calling for his daily visit.

> "And they heard the voice of the LORD God walking in the garden in the cool of the day: and Adam and his wife hid themselves from the presence of the LORD God amongst the trees of the garden. And the LORD God called unto Adam, and said unto him, Where art thou? And he said, I heard thy voice in the garden, and I was afraid, because I was naked;

> *and I hid myself. And he said, Who told thee that thou wast naked? Hast thou eaten of the tree, whereof I commanded thee that thou shouldest not eat?"* (Genesis 3:8-11)

Adam had lost his position of steward, through non-compliance of God's directions, when he ate the forbidden fruit. God called Adam to give an account of his stewardship, and he had no answer. As verse three says, "he couldn't dig and to beg he was ashamed." There was nothing he could do to redeem himself. God still loved Adam and wanted his fellowship, but he could not fellowship with Adam the way that he was. Adam couldn't fix the situation, so if God wanted our fellowship, he had to do something. Adam had no answer, so God himself reveals the answer.

> *"I am resolved what to do, that, when I am put out of the stewardship, they may receive me into their houses."* (Luke 16:4)

God had lost fellowship with man. The reason God made the universe was to fellowship with man. Not only had God lost fellowship with man, but man was now fellowshipping with God's enemy. God began to show man that there was only one way to restore fellowship and reconcile God and man. Man had to see that all other methods fail.

God sent the Law. Did the Law reconcile God and man? No, it revealed man's sin and put them farther away from God. God sent prophets. Did the prophets reconcile God and man? No, man stoned the prophets. The people wanted kings, so God raised up kings. Did kings reconcile God and man? No, the kings taxed the people and brought burdens upon them. God gave priests. Did priests reconcile God and man? No, because it is impossible that the blood of bulls and goats could redeem men from their sin.

When the fullness of time came (the appointed time), God did what he knew that he would do even from the foundation of the world. God took his very best, his Word, and put him in the form of what he wanted to receive: man. Then he sowed him into the ground.

> "Verily, verily, I say unto you, Except a corn of wheat fall into the ground and die, it abideth alone: but if it die, it bringeth forth much fruit." (John 12:24)

When the Father sowed Jesus, he didn't just want Jesus back. He sowed him to get us. We are the increase. The kind of harvest you want determines the kind of seed you sow. God must have had great confidence in the principle he put on the earth—that what you sow, you reap, and you also receive increase.

> "Be not deceived; God is not mocked: for whatsoever a man soweth, that shall he also reap." (Galatians 6:7)

> "Give, and it shall be given unto you; good measure, pressed down, and shaken together, and running over, shall men give into your bosom. For with the same measure that ye mete withal it shall be measured to you again." (Luke 6:38)

Let's examine the greatest gift that has ever been given.

> "For God so loved the world, that he gave his only begotten Son, that whosoever believeth in him should not perish, but have everlasting life." (John 3:16)

Love motivated God to give, but he also gave for a desired result. The Father gave Jesus so he could have us. God gave expecting to receive back what he sowed with increase. He gave so that we might have everlasting life. Love is his motive, but giving is his method.

Love motivated God to give. He loved us and wanted our fellowship. He knew to get what he wanted, he had to sow a seed. We should know the same thing. The love that motivated God produced or worked the faith to believe for the desired result. In this case, that you and I would have everlasting life.

> *"For in Jesus Christ neither circumcision availeth anything, nor uncircumcision; but faith which worketh by love."* (Galatians 5:6)

If giving in order to receive is wrong, then God Almighty was wrong. What about the person who says, "I just want to give out of love and expect nothing back. I just want to please God." Where's the faith in that? This may appear sweet and spiritual at first glance, but the Bible says, "without faith it is impossible to please him" (Heb. 11:6). You see, it is not a choice of love or receiving. It's both or nothing, because faith works by love. The motive of love works the faith to receive the harvest with increase. Without love as your motive, you will fail in your faith to believe and receive the increase.

Did God's seed work? On the third day, God's seed sprouted. Your seed, if you are expecting a harvest, will sprout too. No natural or spiritual force can stop a seed sown in faith. Jesus' body was laid in a tomb, covered by a great rock, sealed with Pilate's seal, and guarded by Pilate's soldiers.

> *"And when Joseph had taken the body, he wrapped it in a clean linen cloth, And laid it in his own new tomb, which he had hewn out in the rock: and he rolled a great stone to the door of the sepulchre, and departed."* (Matthew 27:59-60)

> *"Command therefore that the sepulchre be made sure until the third day, lest his disciples come by night, and steal him away, and say unto the people, He is risen from the dead: so the last error shall be worse than the first. Pilate said unto them, Ye have a watch: go your way, make it as sure as ye can.*

So they went, and made the sepulchre sure, sealing the stone, and setting a watch." (Matthew 27:64-66)

They couldn't stop the resurrection of Jesus Christ, the Son of God. Was he the only one who came up? No, there was increase. Graves opened up all over Jerusalem. He was the first fruits of them who sleep. God sowed a seed in faith and believed when he did he would receive a harvest with increase. He must have believed in his system to give his only begotten son over to it.

"And the graves were opened; and many bodies of the saints which slept arose, And came out of the graves after his resurrection, and went into the holy city, and appeared unto many." (Matthew 27: 52-53)

Jesus replaced Adam, the unjust steward. Adam didn't know what to do, but Jesus did, and the Father was well pleased. Adam, through sin, became an unjust steward. Jesus took his place as the second and last Adam.

"But now is Christ risen from the dead, and become the firstfruits of them that slept. For since by man came death, by man came also the resurrection of the dead. For as in Adam all die, even so in Christ shall all be made alive." (1Corinthians 15:20-22)

"So also is the resurrection of the dead. It is sown in corruption; it is raised in incorruption: It is sown in dishonour; it is raised in glory: it is sown in weakness; it is raised in power: It is sown a natural body; it is raised a spiritual body. There is a natural body, and there is a spiritual body. And so it is written, The first man Adam was made a living soul; the last Adam was made a quickening spirit. Howbeit that was not first which is spiritual, but that which is natural; and afterward that which is spiritual. The first man is of

the earth, earthy: the second man is the Lord from heaven."
(1 Corinthians 15:42-47)

He was still called the unjust steward when he gave away the good things that belonged to the Father. Jesus, who was without sin, actually became the unjust steward by taking on the sins of the world.

"For he hath made him to be sin for us, who knew no sin; that we might be made the righteousness of God in him." (2 Corinthians 5:21)

As the unjust steward, Jesus, was resolved what to do. He gave varying degrees of discounts to the rich man's debtors and gave away the rich man's goods. He gave sight to the blind, health to those that were sick, the ability to walk to those with lame feet, courage to the discouraged, and he gave and he gave.

"How God anointed Jesus of Nazareth with the Holy Ghost and with power: who went about doing good, and healing all that were oppressed of the devil; for God was with him." (Acts: 10:38)

It worked. We love him and his Father (the rich man) commended him.

"We love him, because he first loved us." (1 John 4:19)

"And Jesus, when he was baptized, went up straightway out of the water: and, lo, the heavens were opened unto him, and he saw the Spirit of God descending like a dove, and lighting upon him: And lo a voice from heaven, saying, This is my beloved Son, in whom I am well pleased." (Matthew 3:16-17)

"Then answered Peter, and said unto Jesus, Lord, it is good

for us to be here: if thou wilt, let us make here three tabernacles; one for thee, and one for Moses, and one for Elias. While he yet spake, behold, a bright cloud overshadowed them: and behold a voice out of the cloud, which said, This is my beloved Son, in whom I am well pleased; hear ye him." (Matthew 17:4-5)

Jesus, as the unjust steward, called every one of the rich man's debtors, because no one could pay what was owed. Are we not all a debtor to the Father (the rich man)? Have we not all sinned and fallen short of the glory of God? Some of us may need bigger discounts than others, but none of us can pay what we owe. Thank God that Jesus understands and the Father approves of giving while expecting to receive.

"For all have sinned, and come short of the glory of God; Being justified freely by his grace through the redemption that is in Christ Jesus." (Romans 3:23-24)

In fact, the Father was so pleased with Jesus that he didn't fire him for giving away all his goodness, but instead gave him a raise. He gave him the greatest raise that was ever given.

"Let this mind be in you, which was also in Christ Jesus: Who, being in the form of God, thought it not robbery to be equal with God: But made himself of no reputation, and took upon him the form of a servant, and was made in the likeness of men: And being found in fashion as a man, he humbled himself, and became obedient unto death, even the death of the cross. Wherefore God also hath highly exalted him, and given him a name which is above every name: That at the name of Jesus every knee should bow, of things in heaven, and things in earth, and things under the earth; And that every tongue should confess that Jesus Christ is Lord, to the glory of God

the Father." (Philippians 2:5-11)

Jesus will let us share the fruits of his raise as we become joint heirs with him by grace through faith.

"For by grace are ye saved through faith; and that not of yourselves: it is the gift of God: Not of works, lest any man should boast." (Ephesians 2:8-9)

In the Kingdom of God, when you invest you expect to gain increase. This is not considered as something wrong or ungodly but as something that pleases God and results from godly wisdom.

"And the lord commended the unjust steward, because he had done wisely." (Luke 16:8)

CHAPTER SEVEN

ROLL AWAY THE STONE

Often times, an answer to prayer may be delayed because we first have to do something God has told us to do. The act of obedience in faith is what releases the resurrection power of God to bring a miracle. It will be based on what God has told you to do, not what he has told someone else to do. Let's see how God dealt with a certain widow woman through the prophet Elisha.

> "Now there cried a certain woman of the wives of the sons of the prophets unto Elisha, saying, Thy servant my husband is dead; and thou knowest that thy servant did fear the LORD: and the creditor is come to take unto him my two sons to be bondmen. And Elisha said unto her, What shall I do for thee? tell me, what hast thou in the house? And she said, Thine handmaid hath not anything in the house, save a pot of oil. Then he said, Go, borrow thee vessels abroad of all thy neighbours, even empty vessels; borrow not a few. And when thou art come in, thou shalt shut the door upon thee and upon thy sons, and shalt pour out into all those vessels, and thou shalt set aside that which is full. So she went from him, and shut the door upon her and upon her sons, who brought the vessels

to her; and she poured out. And it came to pass, when the vessels were full, that she said unto her son, Bring me yet a vessel. And he said unto her, There is not a vessel more. And the oil stayed. Then she came and told the man of God. And he said, Go, sell the oil, and pay thy debt, and live thou and thy children of the rest." (2 Kings 4:1-7)

The oil was not multiplied until the vessels were borrowed and brought into the house for the receiving of the oil. The obedience had to come first and then the supernatural could take place. Also notice that God is not interested in what you do with what you don't have. He is interested in your obedience and faithfulness with what is already in your hands. Elisha asked her what she already had in the house. She released it.

"And Moses answered and said, But, behold, they will not believe me, nor hearken unto my voice: for they will say, The LORD hath not appeared unto thee. And the LORD said unto him, What is that in thine hand? And he said, A rod. And he said, Cast it on the ground. And he cast it on the ground, and it became a serpent; and Moses fled from before it." (Exodus 4:1-3).

"For if there be first a willing mind, it is accepted according to that a man hath, and not according to that he hath not." (2 Corinthians 8:12)

The reason why most Christian won't do what God has asked them to do is because they don't think they have the ability to do it. Moses didn't think he could do it. He was right. We can't do what God has asked us to do in our own strength. That's how we know we have heard from God and not our own carnal reasoning. We just offer what we have in the natural and God supplies the power so that our efforts become supernatural as we trust him. God doesn't need our ability, he needs our availability. He has all the ability we will ever need. In his own strength, Moses could not accomplish what God asked him to do. Yet God used Moses and that rod that was already in his hand to deliver his people out of Egypt.

> "For they got not the land in possession by their own sword, neither did their own arm save them: but thy right hand, and thine arm, and the light of thy countenance, because thou hadst a favour unto them." (Psalm 44:3)

God will never ask us to do something that he won't back with his power. As Ethel Waters once said, "God does not sponsor any flops." When God asks us to do something, we must, at least, start out before we see the miracle-working power. Let's see how God used Elisha once again to demonstrate this principle.

> "So the king of Israel went, and the king of Judah, and the king of Edom: and they fetched a compass of seven days' journey: and there was no water for the host, and for the cattle that followed them. And the king of Israel said, Alas! that the LORD hath called these three kings together, to deliver them into the hand of Moab! But Jehoshaphat said, Is there not here a prophet of the LORD, that we may inquire of the LORD by him? And one of the king of Israel's servants answered and said, Here is Elisha the son of Shaphat, which poured water on the hands of Elijah." (2 Kings 3:9-11)

They sought and found Elisha and this is what he said to these kings as the hand of the Lord came upon him when the minstrel played.

> "And he said, Thus saith the LORD, Make this valley full of ditches. For thus saith the LORD, Ye shall not see wind, neither shall ye see rain; yet that valley shall be filled with

water, that ye may drink, both ye, and your cattle, and your beasts. And this is but a light thing in the sight of the LORD: he will deliver the Moabites also into your hand. And ye shall smite every fenced city, and every choice city, and shall fell every good tree, and stop all wells of water, and mar every good piece of land with stones. And it came to pass in the morning, when the meat offering was offered, that, behold, there came water by the way of Edom, and the country was filled with water." (2 Kings 3:16-20)

Without the act of obedience to dig ditches there would have been no water for their needs. Notice that it wasn't God's choice. Whether or not they had water was the result of the kings' choice to make the ditches. The extra oil came from the widow's choice to borrow vessels.

Let's look at the example of Naaman, the captain of the host of the king of Syria, who had leprosy.

"So Naaman came with his horses and with his chariot, and stood at the door of the house of Elisha. And Elisha sent a messenger unto him, saying, Go and wash in the Jordan seven times, and thy flesh shall come again to thee, and thou shalt be clean. But Naaman was wroth, and went away, and said, Behold, I thought, He will surely come out to me, and stand, and call on the name of the LORD his God, and strike his hand over the place, and recover the leper. Are not Abana and Pharpar, rivers of Damascus, better than all the waters of Israel? may I not wash in them, and be clean? So he turned and went away in a rage. And his servants came near, and spake unto him, and said, My father, if the prophet had bid thee do some great thing, wouldest thou not have done it? how much rather then, when he saith to thee, Wash, and be clean? Then went he down, and dipped himself seven times in Jordan, according to the saying of the man of God: and his flesh came again like unto the flesh of a little child, and he was clean. And he returned to the man of God, he and all

his company, and came, and stood before him: and he said, Behold, now I know that there is no God in all earth, but in Israel." (2 Kings 5:9-15)

The cleansing of Naaman's skin was the result of his decision to first dip in the Jordan River seven times. That is how faith works. We do our part first because we believe God's promise. There is no opening the windows of heaven until we decide to first bring the whole tithe into the storehouse.

"Bring ye all the tithes into the storehouse, that there may be meat in mine house, and prove me now herewith, saith the LORD of hosts, if I will not open you the windows of heaven, and pour you out a blessing, that there shall not be room enough to receive it." (Malachi 3:10)

Years ago, I went to church with a woman who said she believed that God had promised to send her a husband. After a while, she said to me, "Brother David, I realized that I wasn't acting in faith toward God's promise of a husband. So I decided to prepare for him. First of all, I am clearing out some closet space so he will have somewhere to hang his clothes."

She prepared her home and made adjustments to enable a husband to move in very smoothly and comfortably. Several weeks later, a man visited our services, and a few months after that he married this lady of faith. She showed her faith first and that moved the hand of God.

You see, this principle applies to today in our new covenant and is not just an Old Testament concept. Consider also Peter and his partner's fishing enterprise on a day when they came up empty.

"And it came to pass, that, as the people pressed upon him to hear the word of God, he stood by the lake of Gennesaret, And saw two ships standing by the lake: but the fishermen

were gone out of them, and were washing their nets. And he entered into one of the ships, which was Simon's, and prayed him that he would thrust out a little from the land. And he sat down, and taught the people out of the ship. Now when he had left speaking, he said unto Simon, Launch out into the deep, and let down your nets for a draught. And Simon answering said unto him, Master, we have toiled all the night, and have taken nothing: nevertheless at thy word I will let down the net. And when they had this done, they inclosed a great multitude of fishes: and their net brake. And they beckoned unto their partners, which were in the other ship, that they should come and help them. And they came, and filled both the ships, so that they began to sink." (Luke 5:1-7)

Jesus instructed Peter (then called Simon) to go into deep waters and then let down his net. It didn't make sense to Peter's natural mind to follow those instructions. They had just finished washing their nets. In addition, they had worked hard all night and didn't catch one fish. Remember, they were professional fishermen. Peter might have thought, Jesus may know preaching, but I know fishing. This was like telling Colonel Sanders how to fry chicken.

However, Peter obeyed. Not because it made sense to his natural mind, but because it was a word from God.

"Nevertheless at thy word I will let down the net."
(Luke 5:5b)

Peter had to obey God first and then came the miracle. If he didn't launch out to the deep and let down the nets, there would have been no fish. Once Peter did what Jesus said to do, the result was a net-breaking, boat-sinking harvest for two boats. If they had ten boats, those would have been filled also. Any limiting factor is always on our end, for God is never limited. If the widow had borrowed more vessels, they too would have been filled with oil.

When God has told you to do something, you must do it first before you see the miracle. Remember that God is a good checker player. When it's your move, he waits.

> "When he had thus spoken, he spat on the ground, and made clay of the spittle, and he anointed the eyes of the blind man with the clay, And said unto him, Go, wash in the pool of Siloam, (which is by interpretation, Sent.) He went his way therefore, and washed, and came seeing." (John 9:6-7)

The man who was blind from birth would remain blind until he followed Jesus' instruction and washed in the pool. There was no vision until there was first obedience. If you want to see a miracle, do something by faith in preparation. Whenever we act on what we know God wants us to do, even though it doesn't make sense in the natural, the act of obedience will release God's resurrection power.

> "Then when Mary was come where Jesus was, and saw him, she fell down at his feet, saying unto him, Lord, if thou hadst been here, my brother had not died. When Jesus therefore saw her weeping, and the Jews also weeping which came with her, he groaned in the spirit, and was troubled, And said, Where have ye laid him? They said unto him, Lord, come and see. Jesus wept. Then said the Jews, Behold how he loved him! And some of them said, Could not this man, which opened the eyes of the blind, have caused that even this man should not have died? Jesus therefore again groaning in himself cometh to the grave. It was a cave, and a stone lay upon it. Jesus said, Take ye away the stone. Martha, the sister of him that was dead, saith unto him, Lord, by this time he stinketh: for he hath been dead four days. Jesus saith unto her, Said I not unto thee, that, if thou wouldest believe, thou shouldest see the glory of God? Then they took away the stone from the place where the dead was laid. And Jesus lifted up his eyes, and said, Father, I thank thee that thou hast heard me. And I knew

that thou hearest me always: but because of the people which stand by I said it, that they may believe that thou hast sent me. And when he thus had spoken, he cried with a loud voice, Lazarus, come forth. And he that was dead came forth, bound hand and foot with graveclothes: and his face was bound about with a napkin. Jesus saith unto them, Loose him, and let him go. Then many of the Jews which came to Mary, and had seen the things which Jesus did, believed on him." (John 11:32-45)

Jesus told them to roll away the stone. Until the stone was rolled away, they would not see the resurrection power of God that can make dead things start to live again. When the people saw the power of God, they believed on Jesus. The same thing will happen in your life when you do what God has told you to do. You will see the resurrection power of God in your life and those around you will believe on Jesus, the Son of the living God.

When Adam lost his fellowship with God, Adam knew he couldn't fix the problem. Because of man's sin nature, we could not reconcile ourselves toward God. It was up to God to act first. Then men could react to what God had already done.

"We love him, because he first loved us." (1 John 4:19)

"For when we were yet without strength, in due time Christ died for the ungodly. For scarcely for a righteous man will one die: yet peradventure for a good man some would even dare to die. But God commendeth his love toward us, in that, while we were yet sinners, Christ died for us. Much more then, being now justified by his blood, we shall be saved from wrath through him." (Romans 5: 6-9)

"That if thou shalt confess with thy mouth the Lord Jesus, and shalt believe in thine heart that God hath raised him from the dead, thou shalt be saved. For with the heart man

believeth unto righteousness; and with the mouth confession is made unto salvation. For the scripture saith, Whosoever believeth on him shall not be ashamed. For there is no difference between the Jew and the Greek: for the same Lord over all is rich unto all that call upon him. For whosoever shall call upon the name of the Lord shall be saved." (Romans 10: 9-13)

Now that Jesus took our sins and received the punishment that we deserved, we move first, not God. That's why Jesus said, "It is finished." God has already given us everything. It is up to us to access them by faith. Notice that the next two Scriptures are stated in the past tense.

"According as his divine power hath given unto us all things that pertain unto life and godliness, through the knowledge of him that hath called us to glory and virtue." (2 Peter 1:3)

"Blessed be the God and Father of our Lord Jesus Christ, who hath blessed us with all spiritual blessings in heavenly places in Christ." (Ephesians 1:3)

Faith moves God. If need moved the hand of God, then nobody would ever be in need because God has an inexhaustible supply of everything good. God has put the kingdom of God inside of us. It is manifested into this three-dimensional, natural world by faith, and it comes from the inside out.

"For, behold, the kingdom of God is within you." (Luke 17:21)

Now, we must act for God to move and faith moves the hand of God. Remember, everything you need to fulfill your kingdom destiny has already been given to you by God. The whole kingdom of God is available to you to access it by faith. All the good things of the kingdom of God are manifested in the natural from the inside out. Since our provision comes from the inside out, then outside circumstances do not affect our provision. Outward circumstances cannot stop us because our provision comes from the kingdom of God that is within us. It doesn't matter if the economy is weak or strong. A bad economy cannot stop your provision, because it's external. It doesn't matter how the economy is or who is in office or what the price of oil is or how high the tax rates get or how much healthcare might cost or if the stock market is up or down. None of these things can change the fact that everything you will ever need has already been given to you and it comes from the inside out.

In review, we must realize that there was no oil until first there was the gathering of vessels. There was no water until first ditches were dug. There was no healing until first the leper dipped seven times. There is no opening of the windows of heaven until the first tenth is given to the Lord. There was no harvest until first the fallow ground was broken up. There was no vision until first there was the washing of the eyes in the pool of Siloam. There was no resurrection power until first the stone was rolled away. There was no Messiah until first the way was prepared.

Let's roll away the stones in our lives. Then what seems dead will come alive and people will believe on the Lord Jesus.

CHAPTER EIGHT

DEFEATING THE GIANTS

Even after we are born again, we still have to turn our thinking from the system of this world if we want to live in the reality of God's kingdom. Even when we receive revelation knowledge that the promises of God are available to us now on the earth, we still have to drive off the giants in our promised land.

As believers, we have the kingdom of God inside of us. God's plan is for the kingdom of God to spread throughout the entire earth through the body of Christ. Once we are born again, the Spirit of God lives inside of us. We come into the kingdom of God and at the same time, the kingdom of God comes inside us.

"Christ in you the hope of glory." (Colossians 1:27)

"And he that keepeth his commandments dwelleth in him, and he in him. And hereby we know that he abideth in us, by the Spirit which he hath given us." (1 John 3:24)

This explains why Jesus said the following in John chapter 14:

> *"Verily, verily, I say unto you, He that believeth on me, the works that I do shall he do also; and greater works than these shall he do; because I go unto my Father"* (John 14:12).

When we enter the kingdom of God, we should know that God has given (past tense) us everything we need while we are on the earth. He has given us wisdom, understanding, health, abundance, peace, joy, protection, and much more. We need these things while we are on earth. Once we get to heaven, our troubles are over. We will automatically have all those wonderful things. Again, they are for us to walk in and demonstrate while we are on earth. That's how we make it on earth as it is in heaven.

There has never been a depression or recession in heaven. In heaven, there is always total abundance. In heaven, we will be walking on streets of pure gold. I heard a joke once that starts with a man standing in front of the gates of pearl taking to Peter. Peter tells the man that he may go back and take one thing from earth to bring with him in heaven. The man goes back and fills a bag with the finest gold on earth. When he returns, Peter looks in his bag and just says one word: "Pavement?"

The Holy Spirit is inside of us to help us access the excess of heaven for every natural and spiritual thing we need. With the kingdom of God inside of us, we don't need to worry about anything. God has already provided everything. That is why Jesus said the following in Matthew chapter 6:

> *"Therefore take no thought, saying, What shall we eat? or, What shall we drink? or, Wherewithal shall we be clothed? (For after all these things do the Gentiles seek:) for your heavenly Father knoweth that ye have need of all these things. But seek ye first the kingdom of God, and his righteousness; and all these things shall be added unto you."* (Matthew 6:31-33)

If we are born again, God has already given us an inheritance. We don't have to wait to walk in it. He wants us to have it now or he wouldn't have given it to us now. We don't have to go to heaven to receive it, for the kingdom of heaven is in you. God wants it done on earth as it is in heaven. Here is the catch. We have an inheritance but there are always giants in the way. It's our job to drive the giants off the land by faith.

This inheritance is already established in heaven and on the earth, but there are giants. There is a battle. This inheritance will not just fall into your lap. Have you noticed that? If it manifested without a battle, then every Christian would be walking in their promised land.

> *"Now faith is the substance of things hoped for, the evidence of things not seen. For by it the elders obtained a good report. Through faith we understand that the worlds were framed by the word of God, so that things which are seen were not made of things which do appear."* (Hebrews 11:1-3)

We must believe that God has already done everything that he is going to do to give us an inheritance. The rest is up to us. God has already promised us and given us the outcome. We just have to walk in it. That's why Jesus made the choice that he did when he chose the last words he spoke with his last breath before he died on the cross.

> *"When Jesus therefore had received the vinegar, he said, It is finished: and he bowed his head, and gave up the ghost."* (John 19:30)

As you begin to use your faith to remove the giants on your promised land (the promises of God), you must first believe that what God has said he has done –He has done. It has already been settled in heaven and on the earth, and now it needs to be settled in your heart and mind. It's time for all believers, in the power of God, to receive what God has already done. It's your turn to move.

God has already moved out of compassion for your need, once and for all. The Father sent his Son for all of humanity. Jesus, the Son of the living God, allowed himself to be stripped of everything so that we might have everything.

He became poor so that we might be rich; he became sick so that we might have health, and he became sin so that we might become righteous. He was rejected of men that we might be accepted in the beloved.

Jesus was stripped of his riches. He was stripped of his glory. He was stripped of his kingship. Then all of our sins, needs, poverty, lack, want, insufficiency, suffering, fear, torment, intimidation, depression, ungodly pride, rejection, bondage, slavery, and debt was placed upon him. Jesus won the victory for us as the perfect, substitutionary sacrifice and, as a result, gained back his throne and kingdom. He has already given up these things for you once, and he won't do it again.

We have a new and better covenant now, and those giants have no right to sit on your land unless you allow it. So let's walk in our inheritance and have the promises of God become manifested in our lives. Let's be like Joshua and Caleb and not like those other ten spies.

The best example of an individual running off a giant is the account of the battle between David and Goliath. I have summarized the story below:

Every day, twice a day, for forty days, the giant, Goliath of Gath, came out of the camp of the Philistines and dared someone from the Israelites' camp to come out and fight with him. He was at least nine-and-one-half feet tall. He wore armor from head to foot, and carried a spear twice as long and as heavy as any other man could hold. Each time he appeared, he called out the same thing across the valley of Elah.

> "And he stood and cried unto the armies of Israel, and said unto them, Why are ye come out to set your battle in array? am not I a Philistine, and ye servants to Saul? choose you a man for you, and let him come down to me. If he be able to fight with me, and to kill me, then will we be your servants: but if I prevail against him, and kill him, then shall ye be our servants, and serve us. And the Philistine said, I defy the armies of Israel this day; give me a man, that we may fight together." (1 Samuel 17:8-10)

On the last day of Goliath's challenges, Jesse, the father of David, sent David with supplies to his three brothers in the army of Israel. As David was talking to his brothers, Goliath came out and issued his challenge once again. The men of Israel told David all about Goliath and his challenges and related how the king will reward the man who kills Goliath with great riches, give him his daughter, and make his family free from taxes in Israel. David decided to accept the challenge and sought out King Saul.

> "And David said to Saul, Let no man's heart fail because of him; thy servant will go and fight with this Philistine. And Saul said to David, Thou art not able to go against this Philistine to fight with him: for thou art but a youth, and he a man of war from his youth. And David said unto Saul, Thy servant kept his father's sheep: and there came a lion, and a bear, and took a lamb out of the flock: And I went out after him, and smote him, and delivered it out of his mouth: and when he arose against me, I caught him by his beard, and smote him, and slew him. Thy servant slew both the lion and the bear: and this uncircumcised Philistine shall be as one of them, seeing he hath defied the armies of the living God. David said moreover, The LORD that delivered me out of the paw of the lion, and out of the paw of the bear, he will deliver me out of the hand of this Philistine. And Saul said unto David, Go, and the LORD be with thee." (1 Samuel 17:32-37)

King Saul gave David his armor to wear in the battle. It would be the way that the world and everyone else does battle. David chose not to wear the king's armor because he had not proved it. It felt cumbersome and unfamiliar. David was skilled with the use of his simple slingshot.

God will use the unique skills he has already placed in your hands, so don't worry about doing things the way everybody else does. Just be yourself and use the proven gifts and talents God has given you. Trust him and he will work miracles through you. Thank God that he does all the hard work. As we trust him, we do what we can and he will do what we can't, like defeat a giant. David took his sling and gathered five smooth stones and then drew near to the giant. Let's finish the story.

> "And when the Philistine looked about, and saw David, he disdained him: for he was but a youth, and ruddy, and of a fair countenance. And the Philistine said unto David, Am I a dog, that thou comest to me with staves? And the Philistine cursed David by his gods. And the Philistine said to David, Come to me, and I will give thy flesh unto the fowls of the air, and to the beasts of the field. Then said David to the Philistine, Thou comest to me with a sword, and with a spear, and with a shield: but I come to thee in the name of the LORD of hosts, the God of the armies of Israel, whom thou hast defied. This day will the LORD deliver thee into mine hand; and I will smite thee, and take thine head from thee; and I will give the carcases of the host of the Philistines this day unto the fowls of the air, and to the wild beasts of the earth; that all the earth may know that there is a God in Israel. And all this assembly shall know that the LORD saveth not with sword and spear: for the battle is the LORD's, and he will give you into our hands. And it came to pass, when the Philistine arose, and came and drew nigh to meet David, that David hasted, and ran toward the army to meet the Philistine. And David put his hand in his bag, and took thence a stone, and slang it, and smote the Philistine in

his forehead, that the stone sunk into his forehead; and he fell upon his face to the earth. So David prevailed over the Philistine with a sling and with a stone, and smote the Philistine, and slew him; but there was no sword in the hand of David. Therefore David ran, and stood upon the Philistine, and took his sword, and drew it out of the sheath thereof, and slew him, and cut off his head therewith. And when the Philistines saw their champion was dead, they fled. And the men of Israel and of Judah arose, and shouted, and pursued the Philistines, until thou come to the valley, and to the gates of Ekron. And the wounded of the Philistines fell down by the way to Shaaraim, even unto Gath, and unto Ekron. And the children of Israel returned from chasing after the Philistines, and they spoiled their tents." (1 Sam. 17:42-53)

David won the battle with the talents and resources that were in his hands. He trusted God to do the rest to bring him a victory over a giant that he could not beat in his own strength. David did not back down or procrastinate. To the contrary, he ran to the battle as his confidence was in the Lord. God's victories are complete victories. The entire Philistine army was defeated and God's people received great spoil.

The big sword in Goliath's hand was a weapon that Satan meant for harm for God's people. If we trust God and hold on to his promise, God will take what the devil meant to harm you and use it to help you get a complete and overwhelming victory. David did not have his own sword. As Goliath lay dead, David picked up Goliath's sword and cut off Goliath's head. At that point, the Israelites chased down the Philistines and the rout was on!

As children of God, we should have the revelation that giants never stopped anyone from entering and enjoying the promises of God. It is the fear of giants that keep many of God's people from walking in their inheritance as children of God. When Moses dispatched twelve spies, one from each tribe, to scout out the land of promise, all of the spies agreed upon the facts. The difference came in their conclusions and recommendations. The conclusions that we make in our life should be based on faith in the Word of God. The revelation that the promises of God are already ours needs to be forever settled in our hearts and mind if we are to run the giants off of our promised land to fulfill our kingdom destiny. We should speak like Joshua and Caleb.

> *"And Caleb stilled the people before Moses, and said, Let us go up at once, and possess it; for we are well able to overcome it."* (Numbers 13:30)

> *"And they spake unto all the company of the children of Israel, saying, The land, which we passed through to search it, is an exceeding good land. If the LORD delight in us, then he will bring us into this land, and give it us; a land which floweth with milk and honey. Only rebel not ye against the LORD, neither fear ye the people of the land; for they are bread for us: their defence is departed from them, and the LORD is with us: fear them not."* (Numbers 14:7-9)

The twelve spies were leaders that had great influence over the rest of the Israelites. The Bible says that ten of the spies gave an evil report.

> *"But the men that went up with him said, We be not able to go up against the people; for they are stronger than we. And they brought up an evil report of the land which they had searched unto the children of Israel, saying, The land, through which we have gone to search it, is a land that eateth up the inhabitants thereof; and all the people that we saw in it are men of a great stature. And there we saw the giants, the sons of Anak, which come of the giants: and we were in our own sight as grasshoppers, and so we were in their sight."* (Numbers 13:31-33)

The report they gave was evil because they took God out of the equation and put themselves in the equation. Joshua and Caleb compared the giants to God, but the others compared the giants to themselves without God. The equation (or inequality) below demonstrates my point.

GOD > GIANTS > Themselves

When they compared themselves to the giants, the giants looked so big that they saw themselves as grasshoppers in the sight of the giants. They didn't see themselves as God does. When Joshua and Caleb compared the giants to God, the giants looked very small. This caused Caleb to conclude that they should go at once and take the land, for they were well able to do it. Notice that it is true that the giants were bigger in physical size than the Israelites. What makes a report evil is to take God out of the equation. Always compare the size of the giants you are fighting against God and the giants will always look small.

There are seven kinds of giants that the enemy will use to oppress you in order to make you afraid to trust God. The Bible tells us of the seven nations that God has already gone before you and cast out. Don't be afraid, for they are bread for us.

> "When the LORD thy God shall bring thee into the land whither thou goest to possess it, and hath cast out many nations before thee, the Hittites, and the Girgashites, and the Amorites, and the Canaanites, and the Perizzites, and the Hivites, and the Jebusites, seven nations greater and mightier than thou; And when the LORD thy God shall deliver them before thee; thou shalt smite them, and utterly destroy them; thou shalt make no covenant with them, nor shew mercy unto them." (Deuteronomy 7:1-2)

Their big, fortified cities, big houses with nice high ceilings and deep wells will be given to you as a blessing from God if you will choose faith instead of fear.

> "And it shall be, when the LORD thy God shall have brought thee into the land which he sware unto thy fathers, to Abraham, to Isaac, and to Jacob, to give thee great and goodly cities, which thou buildedst not, And houses full of all good things, which thou filledst not, and wells digged, which thou diggedst not, vineyards and olive trees, which thou plantedst not; when thou shalt have eaten and be full." (Deuteronomy 6:10-11).

Those seven nations of giants are no match for the power of God. They represent seven evil spirits which are evil counterparts of the seven spirits of God.

> "And I beheld, and, lo, in the midst of the throne and of the four beasts, and in the midst of the elders, stood a Lamb as it had been slain, having seven horns and seven eyes, which are the seven Spirits of God sent forth into all the earth." (Revelation 5:6)

> "And there shall come forth a rod out of the stem of Jesse, and a Branch shall grow out of his roots: And the spirit of the LORD shall rest upon him, the spirit of wisdom and understanding, the spirit of counsel and might, the spirit of knowledge and of the fear of the LORD; And shall make him of quick understanding in the fear of the LORD: and he shall not judge after the sight of his eyes, neither reprove after the hearing of his ears: But with righteousness shall he judge the poor, and reprove with equity for the meek of the earth: and he shall smite the earth with the rod of his mouth, and with the breath of his lips shall he slay the wicked. And righteousness shall be the girdle of his loins, and faithfulness the girdle of his reins." (Isaiah 11:1-5)

Below is a table from Green Light Ministry with an explanation of the evil spirits to be driven off our promised land.1

Table of Evil Spirits

Name	Meaning of Name	Characteristics
Hittites	Sons of Heth (terror) – extreme fear	Death, Fear, Depression, Suicide, Deceit, Purposelessness, terrorism
Girgashites	Clay dweller	Earthliness, Greed, Selfish, fleshly methods, "non-spiritual", stupidity
Amorites	Mountaineer, "Sayer" – one who has a high position from speech	Pride, Fornicator, Possessor, Arrogant, "full of themselves", entrenched unrighteous behavior in the peoples' minds.
Canaanites	Lowland, trafficke in merchandise	Low desires (pleasures), sexual immorality, perversions, homosexuality, non-judgment, spreads evil through pleasure, deceitful affection
Perizzites	Villager (belonging to a poor village)	Small thinking, low self-esteem, poverty, "man" worship (idolatry), ungratefulness, laziness, carelessness, blood-sucking parasite
Hivites	Village people (rich village lifestyle)	Hedonism (life focused on pleasure), purposelessness, fraud, riches, rape
Jebusites	Threshing place (trodden down, and separated)	Legalists, unrighteous judges, racism, class distinction, murderers, spreads death (Hittites) and poverty (Perizzites), hate

We don't have to be afraid of the giants. God has already given us the victory. God drives them out. All we have to do is believe what God has said.

> "He overthrew seven nations in Canaan and gave their land to his people as their inheritance." (Acts 13:19 NIV)

If you are dealing with any of those seven spirits in your life, I declare in the name of Jesus, that through the anointing of God you are set free to walk in your full inheritance for the glory of God.

> *"And it shall come to pass in that day, that his burden shall be taken away from off thy shoulder, and his yoke from off thy neck, and the yoke shall be destroyed because of the anointing."* (Isaiah 10:27)

CHAPTER NINE

ROUTING THE ENEMY

As we saw in the previous chapter, David and Israel won a huge victory over Goliath and the Philistines. This was not rare or unusual. It is the norm for God's people to win an overwhelming supernatural victory that only God can bring. If the enemy has ripped you off or is threatening to rip you off, you keep looking at what you are going to and not what you are going through. Sometimes we can't see what we are going to because we keep looking at what we have been through. We have to let go of the past.

> "Brethren, I count not myself to have apprehended: but this one thing I do, forgetting those things which are behind, and reaching forth unto those things which are before, I press toward the mark for the prize of the high calling of God in Christ Jesus." (Philippians 3:13-14)

Trust God and he will cause you to rout the enemy. Because a youth trusted God, the men of Israel went from shaking in their boots to chasing down the Philistines and spoiling their tents.

God has made a way to recover what the devil has stolen,

and in addition, receive spoil over and above what we've lost. Let's examine how we receive the victory that has already been provided for us by God when Satan has stolen from us. We will also see how to have a great victory even when Satan merely threatens to steal from us. Goliath threatened Israel, but David believed God to produce a total rout.

God has truly made a way for us to dwell under the shadow of his wing and receive continuous protection. He has made a way that by faith we can walk through the waters and the fire and not be drowned or burned. God works all things, even terrible acts of our enemy, to our good if we will trust him. All that is good news, yet each of us have faced or will face loss in this world. I don't know of anyone who has never stepped out of the hiding place of God at some time. Additionally, we can suffer loss from persecution because of what we have done in obedience to God. Elijah's brook dried up as a result of his obedience to the decree that it wouldn't rain unless he declared it so.

We need to know what to do when we suffer loss in this world. If we trust God with the knowledge of what we learn in this chapter, we will recover what we lost with spoil, or God will give us something better to replace it. I don't know how he does it, but he is the God of the impossible. God is smarter than we are and he knows the future. We have to trust him to decide if we recover exactly what we lost with spoil or something different but better than before. In either case, we come out ahead as we trust God. We can even get spoil just because the devil threatens to steal from us.

Many times God restores exactly what we lost plus more of it. That is spoil taken from the enemy. This is what David experienced after he left Ziklag. Remember, recovery could be the same as what you lost plus spoil, or something different but better. It may not seem better at first, but in the end we will see the good hand of God. Let's read a little bit about the story of David at Ziklag.

> "And it came to pass, when David and his men were come to Ziklag on the third day, that the Amalekites had invaded the south, and Ziklag, and smitten Ziklag, and burned it with fire; And had taken the women captives, that were therein: they slew not any, either great or small, but carried them away, and went on their way. So David and his men came to the city, and, behold, it was burned with fire; and their wives, and their sons, and their daughters, were taken captives. Then David and the people that were with him lifted up their voice and wept, until they had no more power to weep. And David's two wives were taken captives, Ahinoam the Jezreelitess, and Abigail the wife of Nabal the Carmelite. And David was greatly distressed; for the people spake of stoning him, because the soul of all the people was grieved, every man for his sons and for his daughters: but David encouraged himself in the LORD his God." (1 Samuel 30: 1-6)

I don't think any of us have ever lost as much as David did. He lost all his family, all of his possessions, and the men were talking about stoning him. At that point, David had no one but the Lord. There was no one to encourage him, so David encouraged himself in the Lord. David worshipped, inquired of the Lord, and received the revelation that God has said we shall, without fail, recover all.

> "And David inquired at the LORD, saying, Shall I pursue after this troop? shall I overtake them? And he answered him, Pursue: for thou shalt surely overtake them, and without fail recover all." (1 Samuel 30: 8)

The Scriptures tell us that David and his men found an Egyptian, a servant to an Amalekite, who was left behind because he was sick. He told David that he was with the Amalikites who invaded Judah and burned Ziklag. Let's pick up the rest of the conversation.

> "And David said to him, Canst thou bring me down to this company? And he said, Swear unto me by God, that thou wilt neither kill me, nor deliver me into the hands of my master, and I will bring thee down to this company. And when he had brought him down, behold, they were spread abroad upon all the earth, eating and drinking, and dancing, because of all the great spoil that they had taken out of the land of the Philistines, and out of the land of Judah. And David smote them from the twilight even unto the evening of the next day: and there escaped not a man of them, save four hundred young men, which rode upon camels, and fled. And David recovered all that the Amalekites had carried away: and David rescued his two wives. And there was nothing lacking to them, neither small nor great, neither sons nor daughters, neither spoil, nor any thing that they had taken to them: David recovered all. And David took all the flocks and the herds, which they drave before those other cattle, and said, This is David's spoil." (1 Samuel 30: 15-20)

David identified the enemy and recovered all with spoil. This is where most Christians miss it and therefore fail to recover all. In fact, if you fail to identify the enemy, instead of things getting better they will just get worse. People are not our enemy. If we come against people, it will just give the devil more of an opening to steal from us. David identified his enemy. He found out that it was the Amalekites who burned Ziklag with fire and stole his family and belongings. We can only recover what was stolen from the person who stole from us. The devil is our enemy, and he is the one who steals from us.

> "The thief cometh not, but for to steal, and to kill, and to destroy." (John 10: 10)

Command the enemy to give back what he has stolen. We need to know that he is afraid of the Jesus in us. We should use the name of Jesus and let God's power do the work.

> *"Recompense to no man evil for evil. Provide things honest in the sight of all men. If it be possible, as much as lieth in you, live peaceably with all men. Dearly beloved, avenge not yourselves, but rather give place unto wrath: for it is written, Vengeance is mine: I will repay, saith the Lord. Therefore if thine enemy hunger, feed him; if he thirst, give him drink: for in so doing thou shalt heap coals of fire on his head. Be not overcome of evil, but overcome evil with good."* (Romans 12: 17-21)

God's word instructs us not to come against people. We should love people, even those who harm us, but we should show no mercy to the devil and his forces. When the enemy steals from us, we should make him pay. People are not our enemy.

> *"For we wrestle not against flesh and blood, but against principalities, against powers, against the rulers of the darkness of this world, against spiritual wickedness in high places."* (Ephesians 6: 12)

David smote the Amalekites. They were the identified enemy. The Amalekites always represent the enemies of God. The Bible says that David smote them from twilight to the evening of the next day. David and his men were tired. They had cried until they had no more power to weep. Then they mounted up and found the Amalekites. They were already exhausted before the battle began. They persevered, because God had said that they would recover all. Even when you're tired, don't quit and you can't lose, because God has said to us in 1 Samuel 30: 8 that we shall recover all without fail. The only way we can lose is if we quit. So, I tell you again. Keep on knocking.

"And let us not be weary in well doing: for in due season we shall reap, if we faint not." (Galatians 6: 9)

For more detail on how to recover what the devil has stolen, please see my book, The Goodness of God. David not only recovered all but he took spoil. This is supposed to be normal for God's people. Command the enemy to give up spoil and expect to receive it. It is ours because we are children of God. Make the devil pay and make him think twice about messing with someone who understands spoil. Remember, spoils may come in the form of something better.

Let's consider the children of Israel in Egypt. They were prospering in the land of Goshen as they lived the way God told them to live (not as the world lived). Many times in Scripture, we see a common cycle for God's people. They obey God and prosper greatly. Then they turn their eyes more on the blessing than on the One who blesses. They end up merging and mixing with the ways of the world. They introduce the world's "gods" into their homes, and it becomes hard to tell God's people from the rest. Eventually, they fall into bondage to the world. In despair, they turn to God, prosper, and the cycle begins again.

Such was the case of God's people in Egypt. Rather than continuing to influence the Egyptians, they were being influenced by the Egyptians. Not only had they been living in Egypt all those years, but, for a long time, Egypt had been living in them. They found themselves in bondage to the taskmasters of Pharaoh, losing their liberty.

The more Pharaoh oppressed the Hebrews, the bigger fall he was headed for when God's people finally turned to God. After Pharaoh's Egypt was riddled by plagues, Pharaoh lost his firstborn son, and finally said to Moses that the Hebrews could leave.

God not only set his people free to live in the land of promise, but he caused his people to leave Egypt with spoil. They stripped the Egyptians of their wealth. Anytime we leave

Egypt (come out of the world system), we receive a total victory. It might look shaky for a while, but if we stand on God's Word, we will rout the enemy and collect the spoil.

The following verses show how the children of Israel obeyed God and took spoil right from the hands of the Egyptians. The wealth moved from the hands of those in the world system into the hands of God's obedient servants. Note that the Hebrew word shaal is incorrectly translated "borrow" in the King James Version in the verses below. Shaal means to ask, request, demand, or require. The Israelites asked or demanded the spoil and the Egyptians complied as they thought of the miracles performed on behalf of God's people.

> "And I will give this people favour in the sight of the Egyptians: and it shall come to pass, that, when ye go, ye shall not go empty: But every woman shall borrow of her neighbour, and of her that sojourneth in her house, jewels of silver, and jewels of gold, and raiment: and ye shall put them upon your sons, and upon your daughters; and ye shall spoil the Egyptians." (Exodus 3:21-22)

> "And the LORD said unto Moses, Yet will I bring one plague more upon Pharaoh, and upon Egypt; afterwards he will let you go hence: when he shall let you go, he shall surely thrust you out hence altogether. Speak now in the ears of the people, and let every man borrow of his neighbour, and every woman of her neighbour, jewels of silver, and jewels of gold. And there shall be a great cry throughout all the land of Egypt, such as there was none like it, nor shall be like it any more. But against any of the children of Israel shall not a dog move his tongue, against man or beast: that ye may know how that the LORD doth put a difference between the Egyptians and Israel." (Exodus 11:1-2, 6-7)

Whenever we decide to come out of the world system to

think and live according to God's principles, our enemy will try to instill fear in us, hoping we will want to turn around and go back. The world system is based on controlling people through fear. If we stand strong and call on the name of the Lord, we shall experience utter and complete victory along with our spoil.

> "And when Pharaoh drew nigh, the children of Israel lifted up their eyes, and, behold, the Egyptians marched after them; and they were sore afraid: and the children of Israel cried out unto the LORD. And they said unto Moses, because there were no graves in Egypt, hast thou taken us away to die in the wilderness? Wherefore hast thou dealt thus with us, to carry us forth out of Egypt? Is not this the word that we did tell thee in Egypt, saying, Let us alone, that we may serve the Egyptians? For it had been better for us to serve the Egyptians, than that we should die in the wilderness. And Moses said unto the people, Fear ye not, stand still, and see the salvation of the LORD, which he will shew to you to day: for the Egyptians whom ye have seen to day, ye shall see them again no more for ever. The LORD shall fight for you, and ye shall hold your peace." (Exodus 14:10-14)

Iran and other nations that want to destroy Israel should think twice about attacking Israel. They should remember the Six Day War. They have been so deceived by the devil that they are blinded by hate and foolishness. My advice to them is this: Don't mess with Israel.

> "And Moses stretched forth his hand over the sea, and the sea returned to his strength when the morning appeared; and the Egyptians fled against it; and the LORD overthrew the Egyptians in the midst of the sea. And the waters returned, and covered the chariots, and the horsemen, and all the host of Pharaoh that came into the sea after them; there remained not so much as one of them. But the children of Israel walked

upon dry land in the midst of the sea; and the waters were a wall unto them on their right hand, and on their left. Thus the LORD saved Israel that day out of the hand of the Egyptians; and Israel saw the Egyptians dead upon the sea shore. And Israel saw that great work which the LORD did upon the Egyptians: and the people feared the LORD, and believed the LORD, and his servant Moses." (Exodus 14:27-31)

My favorite account of biblical spoil is found in 2 Chronicles chapter 20. The enemies of God had to give up spoils just because they threatened God's people. We already looked at what happened in chapter 3 of this book. Let's review the final result as God made a way where there was no way. God's people spoiled the children of Ammon and Moab and the inhabitants of Seir.

"And when Jehoshaphat and his people came to take away the spoil of them, they found among them in abundance both riches with the dead bodies, and precious jewels, which they stripped off for themselves, more than they could carry away: and they were three days in gathering of the spoil, it was so much." (2 Chronicles 20: 25)

God has always desired that a thief not only pay back what was stolen but also give up spoil as part of the thief's restitution.

"If a man shall steal an ox, or a sheep, and kill it, or sell it; he shall restore five oxen for an ox, and four sheep for a sheep. If the theft be certainly found in his hand alive, whether it be ox, or ass, or sheep; he shall restore double." (Exodus 22: 1, 4)

"Men do not despise a thief, if he steal to satisfy his soul when he is hungry; But if he be found, he shall restore sevenfold; he shall give all the substance of his house." (Proverbs 6:30-31)

CHAPTER TEN

JESUS IS THE GREATEST

Former heavy-weight boxing champion Mohamed Ali used to go around saying, "I am the greatest." I submit to you that Mohamed Ali is not the greatest, but Jesus of Nazareth, the Son of the living God, is the greatest. Jesus is the greatest because he is the greatest servant.

> "At the same time came the disciples unto Jesus, saying, Who is the greatest in the kingdom of heaven? And Jesus called a little child unto him, and set him in the midst of them, And said, Verily I say unto you, Except ye be converted, and become as little children, ye shall not enter into the kingdom of heaven. Whosoever therefore shall humble himself as this little child, the same is greatest in the kingdom of heaven." (Matthew 18:1-4)

> "And he came to Capernaum: and being in the house he asked them, What was it that ye disputed among yourselves by the way? But they held their peace: for by the way they had disputed among themselves, who should be the greatest. And he sat down, and called the twelve, and saith unto them, If any man desire to be first, the same shall be last of all, and servant of all." (Mark 9:33-35)

> "And there was also a strife among them, which of them should be accounted the greatest. And he said unto them, The kings of the Gentiles exercise lordship over them; and they that exercise authority upon them are called benefactors. But ye shall not be so: but he that is greatest among you, let him be as the younger; and he that is chief, as he that doth serve. For whether is greater, he that sitteth at meat, or he that serveth? is not he that sitteth at meat? but I am among you as he that serveth." (Luke 22:24-27)

You will either be a servant to God or a servant to sin. Jesus showed us the way. He is our example. We can accomplish things for God on earth because Jesus accomplished things on earth—not as God—but through obeying and serving his heavenly Father. We advance the kingdom of God and bring forth miracles the exact same way. That is, by believing, obeying, and serving our heavenly Father.

> "Let this mind be in you, which was also in Christ Jesus: Who, being in the form of God, thought it not robbery to be equal with God: But made himself of no reputation, and took upon him the form of a servant, and was made in the likeness of men: And being found in fashion as a man, he humbled himself, and became obedient unto death, even the death of the cross. Wherefore God also hath highly exalted him, and given him a name which is above every name." (Philippians 2: 5-9)

We renew our minds to the Word of God and think like Jesus. Even though it is not robbery to see ourselves as joint heirs with Jesus, we humble ourselves as children. We become obedient even to the point of crucifying our flesh. Our heavenly Father then exalts us so that when we use the name of Jesus, the demons and the world obey! We exercise dominion over the world system, not because of our righteousness, but because we have the righteousness of God in Christ Jesus!

> "For he hath made him to be sin for us, who knew no sin; that we might be made the righteousness of God in him." (2 Corinthians 5:21)

Jesus said that if we don't bear our cross and follow after him then we cannot be his disciples. We give our lives to Jesus and instead of losing our lives, we find it. If we try to find our life, we'll lose it, but if we lose our life, we'll find it. Jesus is our example.

> "And Jesus answered them, saying, The hour is come, that the Son of man should be glorified. Verily, verily, I say unto you, Except a corn of wheat fall into the ground and die, it abideth alone: but if it die, it bringeth forth much fruit. He that loveth his life shall lose it; and he that hateth his life in this world shall keep it unto life eternal. If any man serve me, let him follow me; and where I am, there shall also my servant be: if any man serve me, him will my Father honour." (John 12:23-26)

Jesus is the greatest of all time because he is the greatest servant of all time. We should be servants like him. He showed us the way.

> "But Jesus called them unto him, and said, Ye know that the princes of the Gentiles exercise dominion over them, and they that are great exercise authority upon them. But it shall not be so among you: but whosoever will be great among you, let him be your minister; And whosoever will be chief among you, let him be your servant: Even as the Son of man came not to be ministered unto, but to minister, and to give his life a ransom for many." (Matthew 20:25-28)

When we are born again, we become a child of God. We receive an inheritance that is beyond what we can even dream. It would seem to be better for us if we went straight to heaven and all our troubles would be over. No more pain and no more sorrow. We would find everlasting love, peace, joy, abundance, and everything good. Nothing that is bad. Hallelujah!

Have you ever wondered why the redeemed remain on earth to finish their lives?

As a born-again child of God, I am still on the earth to give my life as a ransom for many. I have a race set before me to run so I can bring some other people with me to heaven. If I fulfill my kingdom destiny, my life will have a positive impact on many and the same goes for you! We can be like Jesus as we serve by love. Servants have great faith because faith works by love.

> "For, brethren, ye have been called unto liberty; only use not liberty for an occasion to the flesh, but by love serve one another. For all the law is fulfilled in one word, even in this; Thou shalt love thy neighbour as thyself." (Galatians 5:13-14)

Can a man really follow after Jesus? Yes, but to do so your life must be like that kernel of wheat that falls into the ground and dies as described in John 12:24. You have to want what Jesus wants. Your desires have to be his desires. What Jesus wants more than anything else is see people saved from darkness into his marvelous light.

> "And Jesus said unto him, This day is salvation come to this house, forsomuch as he also is a son of Abraham. For the Son of man is come to seek and to save that which was lost." (Luke 19:9-10)

As believers, we have been given the Spirit of God, the Word of God, the name of Jesus, the authority of Jesus and dominion over the world system. Now, what are we going to do with all that? If we love what Jesus loves, we will give our lives as a ransom for many like the apostle Paul did.

> "For though I be free from all men, yet have I made myself servant unto all, that I might gain the more. And unto the Jews I became as a Jew, that I might gain the Jews; to them that are under the law, as under the law, that I might gain them that are under the law; To them that are without law, as without law, (being not without law to God, but under the law to Christ,) that I might gain them that are without law. To the weak became I as weak, that I might gain the weak: I am made all things to all men, that I might by all means save some." (1 Corinthians 9:19-22)

Jesus is the same yesterday, today, and forever. He will serve us in heaven. Jesus is truly the greatest!

> "Let your loins be girded about, and your lights burning; And ye yourselves like unto men that wait for their lord, when he will return from the wedding; that when he cometh and knocketh, they may open unto him immediately. Blessed are those servants, whom the lord when he cometh shall find watching: verily I say unto you, that he shall gird himself, and make them to sit down to meat, and will come forth and serve them." (Luke 12:35-37)

I will be completely honest with you. Every time I read Luke 12:37, I cannot help but cry. It is overwhelming to think that Jesus will serve us. How I long to be like him. What a mighty, loving, good, perfect, and holy God we serve.

> "Behold, what manner of love the Father hath bestowed upon us, that we should be called the sons of God: therefore the world knoweth us not, because it knew him not. Beloved, now are we the sons of God, and it doth not yet appear what we shall be: but we know that, when he shall appear, we shall be like him; for we shall see him as he is." (1 John 3:1-2)

Jesus is still serving us today. He is constantly making

intercession for us. I have more good news. We have the opportunity to serve Jesus forever. In heaven, we are served as we serve. We give and we receive. God wants it on earth as it is in heaven. How great it is to serve Jesus on earth and how much greater it will be to serve him for all of eternity.

> *"And there shall be no more curse: but the throne of God and of the Lamb shall be in it; and his servants shall serve him: And they shall see his face; and his name shall be in their foreheads. And there shall be no night there; and they need no candle, neither light of the sun; for the Lord God giveth them light: and they shall reign for ever and ever. And he said unto me, These sayings are faithful and true: and the Lord God of the holy prophets sent his angel to shew unto his servants the things which must shortly be done. Behold, I come quickly: blessed is he that keepeth the sayings of the prophecy of this book."* (Revelation 22:3-7)

Let's serve him now and acquire incorruptible crowns. In heaven, everyone will love Jesus. In heaven, everyone will obey Jesus. In heaven, everyone will believe Jesus. In heaven, everyone will serve Jesus. Let's do those things on earth where we can stand out a make a difference to advance the kingdom of God. Then one day we will hear the greatest words that a man, woman, boy or girl can ever hear:

> *"His lord said unto him, Well done, thou good and faithful servant: thou hast been faithful over a few things, I will make thee ruler over many things: enter thou into the joy of thy lord."* (Matthew 25:21).

SUMMARY

How can we serve God while we are on the earth? As discussed, we serve him by love, which produces faith because faith works by love. Without faith it is impossible to please God. To please God, we must believe what he says in his Word. Since we believe his written promises to the righteous (righteousness imputed to us through Christ), we expect to see the manifestation of the promises when we believe and act based on our belief in them.

As a result of our faith in the promises of God, we can boldly approach his throne of grace simply because God said we could. We can also expect to see answers to our prayers and expect to receive harvests containing increase from our gifts to God. We should be constantly expecting the answer or the harvest.

We are so convinced of the faithfulness of God that we keep on asking, seeking, and knocking no matter how long it takes to manifest in the natural. No matter how long it takes, we expect to see results speedily. The longer we wait the closer we are to the answer and the more we anticipate our miracle. We let God decide how he will answer. Our job is to expect an answer when we ask. His job is to answer, and he always does it in the manner and timing that is best for us as we trust him.

We should trust that God is always for us and never against us because everything he does for us is always for our good. We need the revelation that we have a part to play in our destiny. If things need changing, we call the things that are not as though they are. We declare it so in Jesus' name and then the Father makes things on earth as they are in heaven. If we do not make a faith declaration, things will stay the same or get worse.

If the answer to our prayer seems to linger, we examine ourselves to see if we have done everything that God has told us to do. We make sure that God is not waiting on us to obey. If we do need to "roll away the stone," we make sure that we do it immediately. If God is not waiting on us, we continue to look for the answer speedily. Remember, we have to kick the giants off our promised land (the promises of God). We do so by comparing the size of the giants to God and not by comparing them to ourselves.

The longer we wait for our answer the greater the victory and spoil that will be ours. We look at what we are going to and not what we are going through, anticipating that the longer we wait the greater the promotion, increase, and spoil that is waiting for us. As we wait on the answers to prayer, let's be thankful for what God has already given us.

> "He that is faithful in that which is least is faithful also in much: and he that is unjust in the least is unjust also in much." (Luke 16:10)

Let's use what God has already put in our hands to serve others and advance the kingdom of God. As we go through the journey of this earthly life, we serve God and serve others. We give our lives as a ransom for many. Remember, the only way you can lose is to quit. Just keep serving and obeying God. If you don't quit, you will, without fail, be declared a winner by God.

"And let us not be weary in well doing: for in due season we shall reap, if we faint not. As we have therefore opportunity, let us do good unto all men, especially unto them who are of the household of faith." (Galatians 6:9-10)

ENDNOTES

Chapter 8:

Defeating The Giants
http://www.greenlightministry.com/main-article.html

Please visit us at Words of Life Church

David Hope is the Senior Pastor of Words of Life Church, a non-denominational, spirit filled, family church located in Humble, Texas. If you are in the Houston/Humble area please join us for service.

Words of Life Church
7811 FM 1960 Rd. E.
Humble, TX 77346
Service Times:
Sunday Morning 10:40am
Wednesday Evening 7:00pm
Live Steaming Sunday 11:30am
Live Streaming Wednesday 7:30pm
wordsoflifechurch.org or
fb.me/wordsoflife.humble

www.ingramcontent.com/pod-product-compliance
Lightning Source LLC
LaVergne TN
LVHW051608070426
835507LV00021B/2833